Personally dedicated to:

Anyone who doesn't believe
in miracles is not a realist.
David Ben-Gurion
(Founder and first President of Israel)

I thank YOU for this,
that I am wonderfully made;
marvellous are YOUR works;
my soul recognises this.
The Bible

If I want to grasp this miracle,
my mind stands still
stands still in awe.
Christian Fürchtegott Gellert
(German poet, 1715 - 1769)

Günther Kunstmann

WONDERS
are wonderful!

„A miracle is an event
the occurrence of which
cannot be explained.
An event that contradicts the laws of nature
of nature and history,
that should not actually exist.
And yet it did happen."

General definition of "miracle"
Author unknown

Bibliographic information of the German National Library:
The German National Library lists this publication
in the German National Bibliography;
Detailed bibliographic data is available on the Internet at
"http://dnb.dnb.de/"

Title of the original German version:
"Wunder sind wunderbar"
Translated into English
Editorial office: Friends in England

© 2024 Günther Kunstmann, Bamberg / Germany (1)

Die automatisierte Analyse des Werkes, um daraus Informationen insbesondere über Muster,
Trends und Korrelationen gemäß §44b UrhG („Text und Data Mining") zu gewinnen, ist untersagt.
*The automated analysis of the work in order to obtain information, in particular about patterns,
trends and correlations in accordance with §44b UrhG ("text and data mining") is prohibited,*

Cover photography: © 2024 Günther Kunstmann

Editor: Andra Kunstmann, Bamberg / Germany

Publisher: BoD · Books on Demand GmbH,
In de Tarpen 42, 22848 Norderstedt, bod@bod.de
Printed by: Libri Plureos GmbH, Friedensallee 273,
22763 Hamburg

ISBN: 978-3-7693-1617-9

Dedications

For Jesus:
The Son of God and the Son of Man.
The Saviour and Victor of Golgotha.
The glorious conqueror of the devil.
The beginner and perfecter of my faith.
The living Word of God.
The Prince of Peace, eternal God, wonderful counsellor.
Forgiving, comforting, loving and faithful Lord.
...and an infinite number of other names and attributes ...
... my LORD!

Thank YOU,
that I was allowed to get to know YOU. That YOU have forgiven my sins and that I can and will live with YOU for all eternity.
Thank YOU,
that YOU have called me to proclaim YOUR word and to show people this wonderful power of YOUR name.
Thank YOU,
that YOU have filled me with YOUR mighty Holy Spirit, who guides me, teaches me and in whose power I can serve people.
Eternity will not be enough to tell YOU everything and to thank YOU for everything.
HONOUR and THANKS be to YOU - **JESUS** - alone!

For Andra:

You were and are my support, loyal companion for over 43 years, my intercessor and counsellor, motivator, brakeman when I was/am too fast, pusher when I was/am too slow, tester of sometimes daring ideas and much more. Without

you, my life would have been different and much poorer.
Thank you for putting up with me and building me up when I get on your nerves, am frustrated or just can't cope with myself. Forgiving me, being patient, finding the right words for me.
You are a gift from God for my life, a treasure in the most literal sense, a very faithful companion at my side. Blessed is the man who has such a woman at his side! And that's me!
I am happy and grateful that we have experienced all the incredible miracles described in the book together and that you have never left my side. What a treasure of Jesus experience we have received and collected together.

For my mum:

That's what I've called and experienced you as all my life. You cared for me, comforted me, bandaged my wounds, loved me, held me in your arms, prayed for me, brought me up well, taught me the word of God, the Bible, brought me closer to Jesus, set an example for me and others, even today, at the age of 95.
You are a faithful follower of Jesus.
Thank you for everything!

Dad already went ahead to the Lord Jesus in 2018, I am also infinitely grateful to Jesus for him, his example of faith, his strict and righteous upbringing and loving support. Dad → well done, super well done, **thank you**.

For the Jesus Gemeinde (=Church) Bamberg:

Thank you that many of you have been faithfully at our side for so many (or perhaps only a few) years, that you help us to fulfil the vision and mission of Jesus together. We stand together, learn together, pray together, praise and glorify Jesus, defy resistance, experience victories, you have kept our

backs, carried us in prayer, even when we are travelling on the Lord's mission. Faithfully and well holding the fort.
Thank you for your patient love, support and trust.

It's super to see and hear all the miracles and healings that Jesus has already done for you and in the Jesus Gemeinde Bamberg and beyond. You are wonderful brothers and sisters. We still have a lot to experience with Jesus. We are happy to be your shepherds.

For all who are hungry:

for more of the glory of Jesus and the demonstration of HIS power. Pursue HIM and you will experience HIM. You will experience and hear miracles that will be unbelievable. Because JESUS has not changed.
I promise!
And despite all the miracles, it's always about HIM →
JESUS!

Glossary:

The original version is written in German. Some phrases or expressions cannot really be translated.

German humour is also often different to other nations. Please understand it as a "little German lesson".

$\rightarrow$: means that what follows the arrow is a result, a consequence, a logical continuation of the initial sentence or thought.

*: Words marked with * can be found in the glossary with an attempt at an explanation

Claro: a spanish word and means "all clear", "I can see it". It is used in the German slang also.

Suupi: a joking form of "Super".

Ricola: A Swiss company that produces cough sweets and herbal sweets, among other things. It became famous in Germany through its television adverts. "Who invented it? $\rightarrow$ Ricola!". Now it's a frequently used slogan.

Logo: German short form of "logical".

§ 25 StVO = German law: It is the official abbreviation. Paragraph 25 of the German Road Traffic Regulations defines the correct behaviour of pedestrians in traffic.

Queer: means referring to people whose sexual orientation is not heterosexual or sexual orientation is not heterosexual or whose gender identity is not traditionally male or female. Also the LGBT group.

Caravanserai: A **caravanserai** (or **caravansary**) was a roadside inn where travelers (caravaners) could rest and recover from the day's journey. Caravanserais supported the flow of commerce, information and people across the network of trade routes covering Asia, North Africa and Southeast Europe, most notably the Silk Road. Often located along rural roads in the countryside. (Wikipedia)

Sapperlot: "Bamberg slang". A loud, surprised exclamation of astonishment.

Alles Paletti: means "everything is good, ok, perfect, no more questions.

Why don't you write down here your initial thoughts and expectations about the book and title here? At the end you can read it again and find out whether your impressions and expectations were correct. Have fun!

Thoughts about the Cover Photo

Head raised into the dark night sky, eyes scanning the deep darkness with your eyes like a radar beam. 'When' - "Where" - "How will it be"? Expectation, excitement, anticipation is in the air.

And then, a loud 'WUMM' breaks through the tense atmosphere of the viewer. The fireworks have begun. A thin path of light winds its way from the ground into the night sky. Hard to see or follow. And suddenly another loud bang. Before the eyes of the enthusiastic spectators, a gleaming golden 'fire palm' opens up, illuminating the darkness, its embers slowly falling to the ground and burning up like little glowing snowflakes.

'Aah' - "Marvellous" - "Wonderful" - "Incredibly beautiful" - "Fantastic" - 'More! - 'Oooh' !!!
These or similar exclamations may be heard from the audience. People talk about it for a long time afterwards, even though it's just a man-made spectacle. Planned and predictable, subject to the laws of chemistry and physics. A masterpiece of human skill.

You get the impression that this first 'palm tree of fire' has also lit something in the audience's expectations, hearts and emotions. The fuse is burning!
Hunger for more - new explosive colourful light images, the expectation rises.
But it's just a firework display. Over quickly, lots of smoke and bangs, expensive fun and fascination. Man in action and is finite.

But it can also remind us of the miracles of God in this world, in my life and in yours.

We too often look into the darkness of our situation, of our lives. Looking for answers, looking for the light at the end of the tunnel or the horizon. Where could help come from? Who gives us a spark of hope that lights the fuse of expectation and new beginnings?

Unexpectedly, the darkness of need and helplessness is suddenly broken through. Sometimes barely perceptible at first, then it becomes a bright glow, figures, images and colours that you cannot foresee. Only the firework designer knows what he has prepared and ignited.

God is the ultimate firework designer. The inventor of the 'big bang'. Take a look into the depths of our universe with the great celestial telescopes. What a firework show of beauty, majesty, colour and infinity. God's own, self-designed business card.
And all this without photo shop!
And HE loves to set off fireworks of wonders and positive surprises for us, in us and in our lives. And for us it is simply beautiful, staged by a heavenly Father for His beloved children. Just like that.

God himself brings amazing surprises into our lives. They are often simply called WONDERS. They don't just become an exciting event, but life-changing, helpful, groundbreaking and sometimes even life-saving. (Think of the signal rocket on the high seas in distress).

They show you that you are not alone. God is at your side. HE loves you and wants to help you. With HIS inexhaustible possibilities and resources.

Welcome to this book -
a " FIREWORK of testimonies of HIS power"!

If HE ignited it for Andra and me, HE wants to and will also do it for you.

Because everything that God is, HIS love, grace, forgiveness in Jesus, blessings, promises and much more, applies equally to all people. God makes no distinction.
We only have to receive it for ourselves - from HIM.

Why don't you get HIS business card - for ALL cases. HE will gladly give it to you and HE has enough of them.

Personal foreword

Together with my wife Andra, I lead an evangelical independent church in Bamberg / Germany,
the "Jesus Gemeinde Bamberg e.V.".
(www.jesus-gemeinde.de)

We founded it in 1991 and have been the pastors and leaders of this charismatic church from the very beginning.

We have experienced a lot in more than 30 years of church work and ministry in the Kingdom of God, we have grown in faith and in the Word and, among other things, Jesus gave me a prophecy many years ago that I would write books for the Glory of God.
At that time I couldn't relate to this prophecy, let alone imagine it. I have loved reading books since I was a child, but writing them myself was never on my radar.
So I kept this personal word from God in my heart until God brought it out again in 2015 and put it into practice.
And It took so many years for it to become reality.
(so don't give up, even if it takes longer, but don't throw away God's words).

I wrote my first book (!)

' ACTS 29 '

about the signs and wonders that are still happening today, that we should also experience and that Andra and I have experienced and are still experiencing to an increasing extent. The book has now been published in German, English, Spanish and Portuguese and motivates people in different countries and continents to want to experience it too → and they do!

In 2018, God gave me a second book to write,

' WITH JESUS ON PATROL '

which is about empowered prayer, or practising authority in the name of Jesus. We can change many situations in our lives, our city and our country if we intervene and act like 'spiritual policemen' and use our strong 'spiritual authority' that Jesus has given us as His serious followers

My more than 40 years of police service, most of it on patrol duty, was an important part of my training and experience. The book is currently available in German, English and Spanish.
Both books are full of my own personal reports.
To the Glory of the almighty, eternal, living God.
To prove the authenticity and reliability of the Word of God and faith, as well as the power of the name of Jesus.

Jesus has fulfilled his prophecy to me.
I am happy about it, it is fun to write and to review all the events and realisations mentioned.

It's as if Andra and I were once again fully involved in the events described. Repetition, so to speak. And while writing, thanking and praising Jesus for it again and again. Sometimes I marvel myself that I really experienced this and was allowed to experience it. It is an honour for us.

We keep receiving enthusiastic messages about these two books.

Both books are published by BOD - Books on Demand - More on this at the end of the book.

It is important for me to make it clear that miracles are not the only and most important topic of the Bible. All topics of the Word of God are important in their entirety, worthy of study and realisation.

It is about God, Jesus and salvation and a life with which we also arrive at the end of it with our God in eternity.

I don't want to write a theological textbook, but simply shed light on a topic that I think is still underexposed, although it also has its importance. God and miracles cannot be separated, they belong together.

Small and large miracles, preservations, unexpected positive 'coincidences' happen every day, everyone experiences them, but perhaps does not realise it or does not attribute it to God. For example the every breath, the bumblebee or every miracle of faith.

(Note on the bumblebee: At first look, the bumblebee is too big and too heavy, the wings too thin and the wing area too small for it to fly according to the laws of physics. And yet it flies - and how! God has built in a few super - ingenious functions. You can do some research on this).

The whole of creation is a miracle, or rather billions of miracles. And every living thing, plant, physical or chemical law, etc., bears the signature of God. That is why we should also pay attention to the small miracles that God gives us and that make life possible in the first place.

Our body is a masterpiece! Everything works together, is interdependent, interconnected and has enormous capabilities.
Did you know that blood cannot be manufactured? Despite all the progress and technology. Life' only comes from God, the Creator himself.

So miracle after miracle and we take it for granted, we should marvel and be grateful to God every day.

Admittedly, my experiences, which I will describe here in the book, are wonderfully extreme, but a solid wall can only be torn down with big and heavy equipment.

It doesn't always have to be such "big wonders", but we should also hope, trust and believe in real "awesome miracles" alongside the small, medium-sized miracles. NOTHING is impossible for God! Thank God for that.

The 'wall of irrefutable logic' - that's what I'm going after in the book.

It is not the last word in wisdom, because it does the maths without God and closes off many possibilities. That's why I use these examples to shake things up and break down the wall.

Logic is good and God-given, but it often becomes an idol and prevents us from grasping, realising and experiencing things in faith with Jesus.

Quotations without names are from me personally.

Günther & Andra Kunstmann
© Bamberg 2024

The logic of man ends
where the logic of God begins.

God's acts in our lives
are often illogical.

Foreword by Pastor Matthias Jordan

Wonders are wonderful - they confirm the proclaimed word of God and are part of everyday life for believers. Günther Kunstmann's message ignites the hearts of readers and encourages them to reckon with God's miracles every day.

This book reflects exactly what Günther and Andra live in their everyday lives. You can feel the atmosphere of practically applicable faith, the burning love for Jesus and the willingness to always put faith into practice.

We should never be satisfied with just theoretical phrases. Faith without works is dead. Our God wants to prove and show himself practically. In doing so, God wants to use our originality and thus write history with the individual.

It is perceptible that Günther and Andra are always ready to follow the voice of the Holy Spirit. They make themselves dependent on God and count on his miracles.

The reports of the miracles experienced open the hearts of the readers and motivate them to embark on new ventures with Jesus.

Far away from any religiosity, this book shows a way of living authentically, trusting Jesus, following in his footsteps and experiencing real miracles in the journey.

As you read this book, let yourself be ignited anew by the passion for Jesus that can be felt here and broaden your own horizon for the wonderful miracles prepared by God!

Pastor Matthias Jordan
Jesus Centrum Kassel
Germany

Foreword by Pastor Martin Davison

I love it when God sets things up!

I met Gunther and Andra over a decade ago in the Amazonian Jungle of Brazil in a place called Maues. My wife and I have had the joy of their friendship ever since.

Gunther and Andra's new book 'Wonders are wonderful' is born out of a heartfelt desire to see the reader grow into all that God has called them to be, even beyond their wildest dreams or expectations.

You will be drawn into a journey of discovery, where your beliefs and 'logic' will be not only challenged but transformed as you read story after story communicating Gods rich and deep truth in an honest, fun and clear way.

For those of you that know Gunther you will have the sensation of him reading the book to in the comfort of your own home and I guarantee you will laugh as you hear his voice reverberating in your head!

More importantly, I believe the book you hold in your hand will cause you to grow, cause you to desire and expect more, cause you to press into the wonders that 'HE' has prepared in advance for you to walk in......

ENJOY

Pastor Martin Davison
BDS (QUB) Elim UK's International Missions Director
Yate / England

Foreword by Pastor Wilnor Tennant

Get ready for an awakening of your mind as the Power of the Holy Spirit is revealed to you as you read this book.

This book can change your life; gifting you with a greater awareness of how GOD calls us to live in His power and authority.

Günther tells of the many adventures he has been on and the transformative teachings of Gods' Word. Günther entreats to us to come into a greater understanding of the Power of God, and how to walk in the Power of Gods' supernatural. So often we read others accounts of God showing forth in signs and wonders; however for me the account of the 'tour guide' was such a revelation that this book will bring you into a greater understanding of the fullness of Gods supernatural, and the way we can see this in our everyday lives with the outpouring of His glory revealed.

As you read this amazing book, get ready for change in your personal life, as you are encouraged to press into the fullness of all God intends for our lives today.

Pastor Wilnor Tennant
Pastoral Care/ Encourager & Evangelist
Ireland

Foreword by Rev. Mark Irvin

When I read this book from Pastor Günther about wonders my heart to stirred in even a greater measure for miracles even though I have seen many. There are so many more to manifest.

Again it was a wonderful reminder of the keys to supernatural advancement for the Body of Christ to fulfill the great end time commission. The major events of God have always started with a wonder, a "BAM", a "BANG", something that catches attention that a message can be heard, and masses won.

We are living at the end of the Church age, before Jesus comes and when He comes the Church will go out with a bang. The wonders are the bang to catch the attention of a lost world giving the chances to hear what we have to say. It is like a sign of advertisement pointing the observer to Jesus, the way. It was this way for Jesus and remains the same with those that represent him in His name today.

The people did not come alone for the message he gave, but first because of a wonder that they had seen, experienced or heard about. This is what drew the multitudes. Then they came and listened.

The scriptures are full of the supernatural things that are not logical to an unrenewed mind yet are so much the key. One of my Fathers in the faith used to say it this way. Healing and Miracles are the dinner bell to evangelism.

Pastor Günther has written of a few of what he and his wife, Pastor Andra has also experienced, knowing that there are many more to come. He lives in a nation, the nation of German were Martin Luther brought on a reformation, translating the scriptures that had been locked away from common man but now can be freely read and understood.

It is in the Bible that you find the foundation for everything, and in the foundation is the wonders.

This book is packed with many of those scriptures. The wonders of creation. The wonders of the men and women of faith of the Old Testament. The conception and birth of our Saviour Jesus, a wonder. Walking on the water, the multiplying of bread and fish, stopping a storm and these are just a few.

Jesus is our example through his life of wonders of what it looks like for the sons and daughters too really live a supernatural life in a natural world. For Jesus, it was another day in the office. For us God intends the same. And this is the driving force of what Pastor Günther has written.

So what happened to me and I hope the same for you. I am even more inspired, reminded of the basics of the Spirit filled life and why we have this Baptism of Holy Spirit, the Baptism of power.

I see how important it is for people to give their stories and their testimonies as we come together.

Furthermore, I understand how world news and logic can creep in and replaced what is essential in our Churches if we allow it too and lose our hunger for what God has in mind for us.

This book has a great mixture of all. It is power packed with scriptures to show the truth of what is written. The testimonies are astounding and unrenewed mind boggling. The humour and the way it is written is unique and full of humour, I caught myself laughing out loud several tines. I know Pastor Günther and through how he has written this book it brings out his personality in only the way that he can. He's not only has a deep foundation of bible revelation but can bring it out in such a way that the readers and listeners want more.

It is easy to read and understand, yet full of depth. Once you start, if you are like me, you will have to read it through to the end. Your heart will be stirred for more of the supernatural in this natural world.

I want to express my gratitude to Pastor Günther and Andra for allowing us to also experience God through your writings but also a little more of your supernatural life. You have encouraged us to experience more of what God has intended for us to live this life of wonders in this world full of logic.

To the readers, I hope it does the same thing in you that it has in me and I will look forward to hearing some of your testimonies. This book is a wonderful tool for you and me as believers to go forward with this end time move.....

Rev. Mark Irvin
Founder and President of
"From Faith To Faith To The Nations Ministry"
Germany / America and to the Nations

If we bereave the GOD of MIRACLES of HIS miracles, then HE is no longer the God of the Bible.

Table of contents

„You are the God who does wonders;
You have declared Your strength
among the peoples."
Psalms 77 / 14

„For the kingdom of God is not in word
but in power."
1 Corinthians 4 / 20

Introduction

,, And I, brethren, when I came to you,
did not come with excellence of speech or of wisdom
declaring to you the testimony of God.
For I determined not to know anything among you
except Jesus Christ and Him crucified.
I was with you in weakness, in fear, and in much trembling.
And my speech and my preaching were not
with persuasive words of human wisdom,
but in demonstration of the Spirit and of power,
that your faith should not be in the wisdom of men
but in the power of God. "
1 Corinthians 2 / 1 – 5

Over the last few years, our attention has been increasingly drawn by the Holy Spirit to the miracles of God, the mighty practical work of Jesus during his ministry on earth and the outpouring of the Holy Spirit on the first church at Pentecost.

Besides all the other important topics of the Bible, we researched this area more intensively and were surprised how much the Bible speaks about miracles, the working of HIS mighty power , extraordinary signs, angels and this tremendous authority of the name of Jesus - and **ALL of this** was made available to the church through Jesus; rather, Jesus consciously and specifically commissioned the church to bring the message of salvation **AND** this power to people so that they would come to know the God of the Bible and accept Jesus as Saviour.

But not the congregation / church as an institution, but the group of people who have personally accepted Jesus and decided to follow HIM and fulfil HIS mission.

And this group consists of individual people, just like you and me, and those who are yet to come. This is the church of Jesus.

> „(Jesus) *Most assuredly, I say to you,*
> ***he who believes in Me,***
> *the works that I do he will do also;*
> *and greater works than these he will do,*
> *because I go to My Father. "*
> John 14 / 12

Jesus says here **"whoever believes in me"**
→ that is the only condition, not how long you have been in the faith, have a special function or ministry, have attended seminaries, theological universities or Bible schools.
(by the way: this is all super, but still not a prerequisite or necessary qualification)

NO! Just believe in Jesus and do it.

Jesus goes on to say: **"the works"**, not some works → all, to the same extent, without exception, just like Him. Man, that blows my mind - what a mission, what trust in and for us.

JESUS goes to the Father and transfers the continuation of his mighty ministry, in the same strong dimension ...
→ US! → YOU! → ME!
What an honour, privilege and responsibility. WOW!

And this challenges the church of Jesus and every single disciple of Jesus to believe and do it.

Our excitement for Jesus grew, as did our expectation, and we began to put it into practice and pray for people and expect confirmation from God.

What we have experienced so far has been amazing, sometimes unbelievable, but always glorifying JESUS.

Healings without end from the most diverse problems, deliverance from addictions and demonic bondages, changes of situation one after the other.

See "Acts 29", where only a small part of our "miracle experiences" are described.

But as I said, that is not the message or the centre of faith, that is only JESUS. The rest is a God-given, Spirit-worked, word-confirming accessory.

At the same time, we realised again and again that there is currently a great lack and ignorance of this manifested power and knowledge of it in the body of Christ. And not only in Germany, but also in the different countries where we travelled to preach.

Praise God - but there are also many churches that fulfil this mission. Hallelujah!

Where signs and wonders, healings and deliverances happen and they report about it.

And there are probably even more of these churches than you might think.

But still not enough!

In the media or theological opinions and statements, this part of the Word of God, the power of the Holy Spirit, is minimised, negated, described as misleading and sectarian, no longer up-to-date or simply declared to be false.

What a blunder, lack of knowledge or even ignorance!

The miracles are an integral part of God's nature, shown and explained by God Himself, prophets, men and women in the Old Testament, the ministry of Jesus in HIS time on earth, knowledge, boldness and confirmation poured out by the

Holy Spirit, multiplied in the first church until today, experienceable for all who reach out for it and take the Word of God seriously and take God at His word.

Like everything in faith, we should and must CHECK EVERYTHING, even the miracles, because the devil sometimes wants to blind and tempt us with similar things. He acts as if he can play along.

„For false christs and false prophets will rise
and show signs and wonders to deceive,
if possible, even the elect. "
Mark 13 / 22:

„ But there was a certain man called Simon,
who previously practiced sorcery in the city
and astonished the people of Samaria,
claiming that he was someone great,
to whom they all gave heed, from the least to the greatest,
saying, "This man is the great power of God."
And they heeded him because he had astonished them
with his sorceries for a long time. "
Acts 8 / 9 - 11

„And no wonder!
For Satan himself transforms himself into an angel of light.
Therefore it is no great thing
if his ministers also transform themselves
into ministers of righteousness,
whose end will be according to their works. "
2 Corinthians 11 / 14 + 15

„ Test all things; hold fast what is good. "
1 Thessalonians 5 / 21

Just because the devil imitates something to make himself the centre of attention or to make the Word of God look bad, we should not immediately throw everything into the garbage can!

Just because something is perverted, misused or badly imitated does not make the REAL and GOOD worthless.

How stupid or arrogant you have to be to simply not make use of it.

No normal thinking person gives up his driving licence and sells his car just because a few people misuse the car as a getaway vehicle after a robbery or for other crimes.

To be honest, the car is not the problem, but the abuse by man, manipulated by the devil.

You also use sharp knives in the kitchen to prepare your delicious food or to cut and enjoy your big, juicy, butter-tender, 28-day matured, 800 gram Black Angus steak roasted on medium plus with the aroma of eucalyptus charcoal, even though so much harm is done with knives and so many people are killed with them.

It's not the knife's fault. It is a blessing, but like any blessing, it can also be misused and perverted. And unfortunately it is too often.

Or you still pay with cash, with notes, even though you know that they are being faked and put into circulation.
You can easily find out how to recognise counterfeit money.
No   problem   my   friend,   don´t   panic!
Stay calm! Be cool! Var cool, snälla! Bleib geschmeidig! ☺

And please don't make the mistake, like many others, of rejecting God's miracles just because you've heard something that somehow wasn't real. To be honest, you don't do that in your normal life either, so why do it in faith and with God?

Oooh - Buddy! You would miss so much.
Never really getting to know the God of the Bible. Or HIS infinite possibilities - even for you.
never experience Jesus in many areas in which HE is world champion - oops – UNIVERSE CHAMPION !
Experiencing the power of the Holy Spirit, HE loves doing miracles because it is completely normal for HIM. And I also believe that He really enjoys it.

Don't let yourself be fooled, deceived, lied to, discouraged or otherwise dragged down.

That's why we have received the Holy Spirit from God, who gives us the gift of discernment of spirits, among other things.
(1 Corinthians 12 / 7 - 11)
You can know where something comes from.

There are miracles that are real. Wanted and made by God himself. Millions of them - in the past, TODAY and they will still happen tomorrow again and again. Even more. God will step on the gas! Accelerate!

It's also written in the Bible dozens of times. From front to back. We can't ignore it. Pretend it's all FAKE. Then we would be making a liar out of God and Jesus. Let that be far from us!

The devil hates these miracles and the knowledge and revelation about them because they make him look pale. He cannot touch this power of God.
He gnashes his teeth, breaks out in a sweat and weakens his

knees when he sees how the Holy Spirit explains it to you and you start to see it, believe it and do it.

Then Mr Dark, the loser of Golgotha, the old snake with the crushed head, the devil, sees his hope dashed.

If you are already a Christian, stand up in faith, be bold and show it to the devil so he knows the score!
Now more than ever! Show him, the eternal loser, the old snake, the cheat and murderer!
Show him the power of the Holy Spirit and the name of Jesus who defeated him. Completely, totally, for eeeeeever!
Show him that you believe Jesus and his word more than him. That miracles are real!

And if you are not yet a Christian in the sense of the Bible, then please read on, marvel and wait for your chapter, it will come soon. I promise.

And it stays that way:

**God says and writes what he means
and HE also means what HE says or writes.
HE is as HE is and was,
HE never changes.**

And that is why there is hope for our countries and our churches, because the Holy Spirit is in the process of reviving this dimension from John 14/12 (see above, you know: doing the same works!) in his body.
There will be another mighty outpouring of the Holy Spirit on earth before Jesus returns.

Just as they have done before, in many countries, over the centuries, such as on Azusa Street in Los Angeles from 1906 to 1908 and many other places in recent history.

Many apostles will rise up again in the land, as in the time of the Acts of the Apostles. Today they have pretty much disappeared from our spiritual landscape, from the churches.

We have many leaders with titles, functions and positions. Just job descriptions.

But it's almost as if people are afraid to call this calling of God so publicly. Apostle.

But where are the apostles?
Equipped with a supernatural power that amazes the world?
Acting with supernatural wisdom and knowledge because they are full of the Holy Spirit and faith?
That you hear about? In the churches, the news, city council meetings, etc.?
For whom the whole nation has respect and esteem?

„And through the hands of the apostles
many signs and wonders were done among the people.
And they were all with one accord in Solomon's Porch.
Yet none of the rest dared join them,
but the people esteemed them highly.
And believers were increasingly added to the Lord,
multitudes of both men and women,
so that they brought the sick out into the streets
and laid them on beds and couches,
that at least the shadow of Peter
passing by might fall on some of them.
Also a multitude gathered from the surrounding cities
to Jerusalem, bringing sick people
and those who were tormented by unclean spirits,
and they were all healed. "
Acts 5 / 12 – 16

„Then fear came upon every soul,
and many wonders and signs
were done through the apostles. "
Acts 2 / 43

„And with great power
the apostles gave witness
to the resurrection of the Lord Jesus.
And great grace was upon them all. "
Acts 4 / 33

Apostles in Action – WOW!

The apostles will come forth again because the Word of God says that HE has given them to the church.

„And He Himself gave some to be apostles,
some prophets, some evangelists,
and some pastors and teachers,
for the equipping of the saints
for the work of ministry,
for the edifying of the body of Christ,... "
Ephesians 4 / 11 + 12

But we still hear too little about it in the country.

Unfortunately, you don't read anything about reports of faith, miracles and healings on the websites of many different churches. Lots of other good information, programmes, groups, invitations. Often very well presented. Also important.

But little of what Jesus does in people's lives. And that is so important.

What is happening or changing in my life or the lives of others?

Good news that raises hope.

Life reports, daily intervention by God, miracles! Not just theologically sophisticated sermons.

There's nothing to be said against it - sermons should be good, realistic, challenging and realisable for everyone.

But without these "testimonies" it is actually a great pity, because something very important is missing, and yet it is actually provided by the Holy Spirit!

Faith must be demonstrated in practice, not just in theory.

To be experienced by everyone. Contagious. Inspiring. Changing for the better.

Just "wonderful".

People are looking for answers, help and hope for miracles as a last solution.

Everyone knows what our neighbours and colleagues say in everyday language:

"Only a miracle can help"

"If only a miracle could happen now!"

"Only a miracle can save me now"

Man instinctively senses, placed in every human heart by God, that there is only supernatural help for certain things. It only works with a miracle.

And he waits for someone to introduce him to this divine help, to tell him about it and point it out.

This book aims to encourage, to awaken hunger, to make people marvel, to draw them closer to Jesus and his word, to create a longing to experience with Jesus these dimensions of power, miracles and healings, the ministry of angels and much more, according to the word of God, and to serve other people so that they too can come to know Jesus.

It's not just about big miracles, as we run the risk of overlooking or underestimating the small miracles of God that we experience every day. We need both - small and big miracles of God, because miracles always challenge our human logic.
Logic is good - but not everything with God. God has his own logic. And what is often logical for God is not comprehensible for humans. It can only be grasped and experienced through "faith".

The expression "a miracle" always elicits an inner smile from me at the lack of logic; because every minute we see miracles and nothing but miracles.

Otto von Bismarck
He was the first Chancellor of the German Empire
from 1871 to 1890

It is illogical to think that logic is the only imaginable possibility.
Georg-Wilhelm Exler

This book will help you to discover it!

YOU - who are already a Christian,
to enter into this realm of the Word of God, to gain knowledge and new courage, to dare to do so and to experience miracles yourself.

YOU - who do not yet know Jesus,
to read that there is hope and a God who wants to show himself to YOU in an unchanged form, that HE loves you and wants to help YOU. You are not lost yet!
God's possibilities are unimaginable and infinite.

And we pray that it will encourage YOU and bring YOU deeper into the Word of God, so that faith will grow in YOU, that YOU will count more and more on the supernatural intervention of God.

All the reports described here are true, even if they sound "unbelievable", we have experienced everything ourselves and most of them have been witnessed by other people.

I, Günther, am mainly writing this book, but it is "our" book, Andra's and mine, because we have experienced most of the reports together, we are of the same opinion in the explanations, we both cannot be separated and we have received a common ministry of proclamation from God.

Have fun, be amazed and become hungry for more of JESUS as you read, reflect and prove the Word of God ...

... GOD Bless you from the bottom of our hearts

Günther & Andra Kunstmann
Pastors of Jesus Gemeinde Bamberg / Germany
www.jesus-gemeinde.de
© Bamberg, 2024

Wonders are wonderful

There is no other way to describe it.
When I was writing this book, I prayed and asked Jesus what title HE had for the book.
HE gave me this title.

"Wonderful" is a very special word.
Positive, creating joy and enthusiasm. Mysterious, building suspense. Expectation of the explanation.
A word of positive superlatives. Where there is almost no increase. It is not just "good" or "beautiful", it combines something experienced with a circumstance that works or is like a miracle.
It ignites a firework of enthusiasm in your imagination and feelings, releases happiness hormones and seeks to express the mental enthusiasm through your tongue and lips, leaving hope and certainty in your life.

You look at the mountain panorama of the Dolomites/Italy in the evening sun, the rocks seem to glow, sublime, majestic, eternal. All in colours that no human could ever paint like this. Constant change, sometimes only in nuances, sometimes blatant.
Your first word is probably "wonderful".

Or you're sitting on your little island in the South Seas or the Caribbean, comfortable in a deckchair, your toes digging in the warm, snow-white, fine-grained sand, looking out over crystal-clear, turquoise-coloured water that ripples gently in the balmy, pleasant breeze, the occasional fish jumping out of the water, close enough to touch and winking at you. In your hand is a fresh, chilled coconut, from which you savour the coconut water through the natural straw. Your gaze goes to the horizon, where the glowing red sun is sinking into the sea as a huge fireball.

You can only breathe a reverent "heavenly"! Right?

In this state of mind we realise again and again that our words often cannot adequately describe what we are seeing and feeling.
Earth meets sky. The natural meets the supernatural. Man meets the mighty God. The creator. The inventor of eternity and the endless universe, of colours, of fantasy, of unspeakable perfection. And our little language centre does not come close to this divine dimension of glory. It is helpless. You rummage through your eloquence box. Searching for words and expression - in vain → and that's why we breathe a stunned

" wonderful "

or

"heavenly"
" glorious "
"marvellous"
"inconceivable"
"unimaginable"

these are similar words.

"Heavenly" - what do you mean by that? What do you have in mind?
Do you know what it looks like in "heaven", eternity with God, Jesus and the Holy Spirit? Even the Bible only gives a rudimentary description because our little grey cells, our barely 1.5 kilograms of brain mass, cannot absorb or process it at all. They would run hot, overheat, switch on the red warning light and beg to cool down.

So God just leaves it at that, gives a few tips to maximise the anticipation and tense expectation.

And so at the moment it remains an indefinable - but we associate it with "Super - Perfect - Great - Whoopee!", dimension and imagination, tingling hope and almost unbearable expectation and we end up back at WONDERFUL and Co!

The same with " glorious".

"Incomprehensible and unimaginable" - why do you even try it? Our human, earthly, limited brain is already waving the white flag again!
Capitulation of the imagination. "Error", "Game over", "Restart required".
Send an error message? But where to?

It is from another dimension. The supernatural, eternal kingdom of God.
I can imagine that God uses these words very often because HE is in the midst of GLORY.
It is everyday vocabulary for HIM. ☺

On further reflection, I realised that I had almost never thought about what ''wonder'' or '' wonderful'' etc. (see above) actually means.

You know it roughly, but have never really reflected on it consciously and in detail. I just use it where I think it fits. It will fit – may be!

Unfortunately, we don't think enough about language, expression and content today. We have largely become superficial as a society.

And that shouldn't be the case.

So here then is the very deliberate question:

Why are "wonders are wonderful" :

- you can't explain them
- they come as a surprise
- they are always positive
- they help
- they heal, contrary to or despite medical diagnoses
- they change circumstances
- they prevent disasters
- they save, even in the most literal sense
- they encourage, give hope
- show that the God of the Bible really does exist
- reveal to us the omnipotence of this God
- reveal to us that we do not have to be alone
- are an invitation from God to trust HIM
- are the "ID card" of Jesus! HIS ID – Card
- make us hungry and want more of it
- do not need many words
- are not a coincidence, but intentional
- can change lives and attitudes
- ...
- …

I don't think the list is complete yet and could become quite long.
You can write down what else you can think of yourself.

Oh yes, I want to explain briefly about Jesus' ID card. I don't want you to have sleepless nights wondering where on earth Jesus got his ID card.

This ID card comes directly from the desk of the King of all kings, the God of all gods, the eternal Majesty from the Kingdom of God, from the Father of Jesus.
Certainly with signature, stamp and an official seal. A really

laaaarge official seal. That's the way it should be.

GOD guarantees this.

> *,,And it shall come to pass*
> *That whoever calls on the name of the* LORD
> *Shall be saved.*
> *Men of Israel, hear these words:*
> *Jesus of Nazareth,*
> *a Man attested by God to you*
> *by miracles, wonders, and signs*
> *which God did through Him in your midst,*
> *as you yourselves also know... "*
> Acts 2 / 21 + 22
> (A passage from the Apostle Peter's Pentecost sermon)

God performs mighty miracles through Jesus → the people experience these → and God "proves" in the sense of "identification" that everything is real → and Peter reminds the people of this.

The miracles are the proof = the ID-Card. God confirms Jesus through the miracles.

> ,,Hey friends! Why don't you remember
> how you experienced this Jesus.
> How many of you here have experienced through Jesus
> healing or deliverance through Jesus?
> **Raise your hand please!!!**
>
> **WOW! Praise Jesus! That's thousands!**
>
> Thank you - you can put your hands down again.
> So you know what I'm talking about - right?
> Jesus could only do that,
> because God was behind him and wanted it that way.
> 100 %.

It was all real, live and in colour, no fake.
No cheap card player tricks."

That's how I imagine the scene. Most people nodded,
agreeing with what Peter had just said.

And we get the same " ID card" if we believe God and do
what he says.

> *„And he (Jesus) said to them,*
> *Go into all the world*
> *and preach the gospel to every creature.*
> *He who believes and is baptized will be saved;*
> *but he who does not believe will be condemned.*
> *And these signs will follow those who believe:*
> (note: will! it will not fail, 100 %)

> ***In My name they will cast out demons;***
> ***they will speak with new tongues;***
> ***they will take up serpents;***
> ***and if they drink anything deadly,***
> ***it will by no means hurt them;***
> ***they will lay hands on the sick, and they will recover.***

> *So then, after the Lord had spoken to them,*
> *He was received up into heaven,*
> *and sat down at the right hand of God.*

> ***And they went out and preached everywhere,***
> ***the Lord working with them***
> ***and confirming the word***
> ***through the accompanying signs. "***
> Mark 16 / 15 – 20

God confirmed it again (!)
with miracles, healings and extraordinary signs.

Super. That's how he is!

Exactly THESE signs happened as confirmation of which Jesus had just spoken, or rather - promised, promised. Jesus keeps HIS word, we sometimes (often?) don't.

Sorry - so WE (!) have to ask ourselves or put up with the question, do these signs also happen in my and your life as a Christian?

Actually, they should.

If not or not yet everything, we MUST, and I say this deliberately, ask: WHY NOT?

A little help with the answer: It is not because of God and Jesus or the Word of God! It has already been written and said unalterably and has been experienced and confirmed millions of times.
As I said - SORRY!

God can be experienced. HE loves to perform miracles. It is HIS nature, HIS character, HIS signature, HIS proof of love for you and me.

And this is still the case today. Big and small wonders. Some that are easy to overlook and others that literally knock your socks off.
The Never - Ending - Love - Story → with miracles. It doesn't work WITHOUT and HE doesn't want it WITHOUT.

„Most assuredly,
I say to you, he who believes in Me,
the works that I do he will do also;
and greater works than these he will do,
because I go to My Father. "
John 14 / 12

I love this passage and can't repeat it often enough because it speaks about me and you (if you already believe in Jesus)

Plain and simple. Without ifs and buts. Without a loophole. Understandable for everyone, even without theological background or frills and small print.

Mamma Mia - what a dimension, what an adventure there is to discover and experience. How many years had I overlooked it, not heard it and not even realised it?

And Jesus says it unmistakably to HIS followers. No debate, excuse, misunderstanding.

"Whoever believes in ME (Jesus) ..."
Please only believe in J E S U S - not in a church or doctrine or anything pious or religious or other persons.
Simply JESUS - as HE lives and breathes and is described and shown to us in the Bible. How the Holy Spirit reveals HIM.

Not how people interpret Him, want to see Him, pervert Him, try to explain or refute Him. (there's an artist today in Germany who portrays Jesus as a homosexual and even organises exhibitions - Mamma Mia! - What a blasphemy).

Jesus loves this guy just as much, that's so amazing and great. Some people only recognise Jesus, the saviour and liberator, later - or not at all?

Only Jesus!!!!

He is enough and everything!

Genial. Simple. Yippie!

„Likewise, I say to you,
there is joy in the presence of the angels of God
over one sinner who repents."
Luke 15 / 10

That is the BIGGEST MIRACLE of all.

When a person realises that he is lost and needs salvation. Realises that he cannot impress God through his own performance, being good, social behaviour, religious or similar.
But he realises that only by accepting Jesus will he go to heaven. But I don't want to anticipate everything here, otherwise there will only be blank pages in the middle of the book. It doesn't look good either. So be patient a little longer.

When a person is healed or set free, when mighty miracles happen, as for example written here in the book, then all this is no reason for the angel team to open a barrel, to rejoice, celebrate and have great joy.

Because these "actions" are normal in the kingdom of God and happen all the time.

But a person repents, that is, he realises that he has been totally wrong, has completely missed the mark and life, missed the target - and then turns back.

It's a miracle that makes even the angels jump for joy.

God's favourite miracle is
when a person recognises
and accepts Jesus
and is saved as a result.

Blind eyes are opened

In 2018, Andra and I were invited to a healing seminar at Apostle Raúl Reyes' church, "Un Estilo de Vida" in La Plata, Argentina. We were to spend a whole weekend there teaching and praying for people on the subject of "Healing in the name of Jesus". Hundreds of people came to hear and experience the word of God in this area.
It was a strong anointing of the Holy Spirit on this special weekend and we were excited to see what would happen.

And Jesus confirmed his word, which we had taught and preached according to Mark 16 / 20:

„But they (Günther and Andra) went out
and preached everywhere,
(that means La Plata / Argentina, among others)
with the co-operation of the Lord,
confirming the word
through the signs that took place."

Do you remember? ID-Card from God and all that?

Hundreds of healings took place, which many people witnessed at the seminar or in the weeks that followed. With every testimony, hope and faith in Jesus grew. There was an excitement, an enthusiasm among the people, the noise level was often so high that you could no longer understand your own words, let alone the prayer requests of the individuals.
And yet we prayed for the people because Jesus knew what was needed.

A woman came to me for prayer with her boy, who was about 9 years old, told me something amidst all this noise and pointed to her boy.
I understood that the son had some kind of problem, but had

no idea what it was and prayed for him.
Completely unspectacular, completely unknowing, but full of faith in Jesus and HIS healing power.

The mum left with her son afterwards. I thought I'd never see her again. No way!

Two weeks later we were back in this church to minister again with the Word of God and prayer.

The mother and her boy were there again, and this time even the father was there.
She told me (it was much quieter, we could communicate ☺) that she had come forward to pray because her son had been born with a blind left eye and now, in the healing seminar, she had the hope that Jesus would heal the eye. After I had prayed for the boy, they went home. Apparently nothing had happened, everything was the same. The eye was blind.

The next day, the boy came to his mother and said: "Mum, I can see something with my blind eye!"

"No my boy, you're wrong, the eye is blind" was the mother's reply. The boy didn't give in and kept repeating his statement that he could see something with his blind eye, it had never been like that before.
The mother initially held on to her knowledge and conviction that one eye had been blind since birth.
In the end, the boy's persistence made her suspicious and she carried out a few simple tests with him and realised that something was different now and that he really could see something. Could something have happened during the healing prayer?

So they went to the ophthalmologist they had always seen and the doctor examined the boy's left eye.

His result was that the boy now had about 30 percent vision in his blind eye. He couldn't explain this because the boy was born blind in that eye and he knew him.

The doctor sent the woman and her son home again, telling them to keep an eye on the situation and report back to him and that there was nothing more he could do at the moment.

Over the course of the week, his eyesight got better and better and they decided to go back to the ophthalmologist.
A further specialist examination revealed that the boy had 100 percent eyesight in both eyes.
What a surprise for the doctor and the woman testified to him about the healing prayer and the intervention of Jesus.

I was totally excited about this healing report, shouted out a "Gloria Jesús" and was about to say a prayer of thanks with the woman when she interrupted me.

"I'm not finished yet, the bombshell is still coming!"
I looked at her a little perplexed, but excitedly.

"My husband, the boy's father, was also born with a blind eye, but on the other side, on the right. He has never been able to see anything with that eye.
He was not present at the healing prayer, but when the healing process began with our son, he also realised that he could see something in his blind right eye. Over the course of the week it got better and better. He also went to the ophthalmologist and he confirmed that he had about 80 percent eyesight in his previously totally blind eye, up to the present time.
We believe and trust that Jesus will also complete here what HE has begun"

I was totally surprised by this report, but of course completely thrilled and grateful.

Jesus surprised us all. But He is often like that. ☺

Over the past few years, Jesus has led us more and more, deeper and more intensively into this very important aspect of the kingdom of God.
The more we study in the Word, recognise God's nature and actions, look at the ministry of Jesus in his time here on earth, see the first church as described in the book of Acts, we realise that all this happened with a tremendous dimension of power, signs, wonders and healings that everyone in the area was talking about.

> *,, Men of Israel, hear these words:*
> *Jesus of Nazareth,*
> ***a Man attested by God to you***
> ***by miracles, wonders, and signs***
> *which God did through Him in your midst,*
> *as you yourselves also know ... "*
> Acts 2 / 22
> (A passage from the Apostle Peter's Pentecost sermon)

> *,, And there are also many other things that Jesus did,*
> *which if they were written one by one,*
> *I suppose that even the world itself*
> *could not contain the books that would be written. "*
> John 21 / 25
> (that's a bold statement - isn't it?)

> *,, And he (Jesus) came down with them*
> *and stood on a level place with a crowd of His disciples*
> *and a great multitude of people*
> *from all Judea and Jerusalem,*
> *and from the seacoast of Tyre and Sidon,*
> ***who came to hear Him and be healed of their diseases,***
> ***as well as those ...***

... who were tormented with unclean spirits.
And they were healed.
And the whole multitude sought to touch Him,
for power went out from Him and healed them all. "
Luke 6 / 17 - 19

„ Then Jesus went about all the cities and villages,
teaching in their synagogues,
preaching the gospel of the kingdom,
and healing every sickness and every disease
among the people. "
Matthew 9 / 35

„ Also a multitude
gathered from the surrounding cities to Jerusalem, **bringing**
sick people
and those who were tormented by unclean spirits,
and they were all healed. "
Acts 5 / 16
(this was done by the first church
and this angered the religious leaders
because it disgraced their position of power and theology
and questioned it, and that is not acceptable!
Read in Acts 5 what happens next.
But fasten your seatbelt and hold on tight!)

As Jesus and His Father, the God of the Bible, never change,
but were, are and will always be the same, He will always do
the same through the Holy Spirit.
That is His will, His character, His expression of love for us
humans.

„Jesus Christ is the same
yesterday, today, and forever. "
Hebrews 13 / 8

And we cannot and will not deny, ignore, minimise or otherwise negate this. That's just the way it is.

Even if it makes Christian leaders nervous and aggressive. Unfortunately, nothing has changed. They are fighting for their small, miserable empire.

But God's kingdom is power, miracles as confirmation of the word. Everything else is not God's kingdom, even if it may be called "God's kingdom". NO – it´s not.

You cannot and should not separate God from HIS miracles.

And as the body of Jesus, we should, can, may and must return to this dimension in order to show people the love of God and HIS unlimited power and possibilities in the current final phase of world history. Into the dimension of the "unimaginable".

Miracles will and can happen that we could never even have imagined.

„But as it is written:
Eye has not seen,
nor ear heard,
Nor have entered into the heart of man
The things which God has prepared
for those who love Him.
But God has revealed them to us through His Spirit.
For the Spirit searches all things,
yes, the deep things of God.
For what man knows the things of a man
except the spirit of the man which is in him?
Even so no one knows the things of God
except the Spirit of God.
Now we have received, not the spirit of the world,
but the Spirit who is from God,
that we might know the things
that have been freely given to us by God. "
1 Corinthians 2 / 9 – 12

Personally, I realise that I still have too little idea of the possibilities of God and what I have been "given by God".

I earnestly ask the Holy Spirit to bring me into this dimension of the "unimaginable", "never before heard or seen". Into this "given by God".

If God gives it to us, we should accept it, unpack it, use it, enjoy it and rejoice in our loving, gift-giving Father in heaven.
And only for HIS HONOUR. (not mine!)
So theoretically I already know because it's in the Word of God. I had heard and read it often enough.

I know:
- GOD can do EVERYTHING
- GOD is unlimited
- GOD is, among other things, power → Dynamis! (ahem - does that ring a bell? Dynamite and all that?)
- I read about the miracles that Jesus performed
- and the mighty things that God already showed in the Old Testament

so far all claro*, check, suupi* ☺ ...

... but do I really expect it TODAY?
- in my life - in a very practical way?
- the same, incredible dimension?
- in our church and our ministry?
- through me?
- Miracles we hear about on the evening news?
- Raising the dead?
- Crowds of people coming together to see and experience for themselves?
- and thereby accept Jesus as Lord?

I need help from the Holy Spirit to really believe it, to even begin to imagine it and, above all, to expect it.

Because sometimes I realise that my faith is really just an agreement, a recognition of the truth, but not yet a creative conviction that moves something, as it is defined in the letter of Hebrews 11 / 1.
And I am convinced that the church of Jesus worldwide, regardless of its colour, does too.

I want to see and experience - and if possible everything - that Jesus said to his disciples, that the first church in the Book of Acts experienced and that has been experienced again and again by Jesus' disciples over the centuries.

„And when He had called His twelve disciples to Him,
He gave them power over unclean spirits,
to cast them out,
and to heal all kinds of sickness and all kinds of disease. "
Matthew 10 / 1

„And as you go, preach, saying,
The kingdom of heaven is at hand.
Heal the sick,
cleanse the lepers,
raise the dead,
cast out demons.
Freely you have received, freely give. "
Matthew 10 / 7 + 8

„ Therefore those who were scattered
(the disciples who were expelled from Jerusalem and fled)
went everywhere preaching the word.
Then Philip went down to the city of Samaria
and preached Christ to them.
And the multitudes with one accord ...

… heeded the things spoken by Philip,
hearing and seeing the miracles which he did.
For unclean spirits, crying with a loud voice,
came out of many who were possessed;
and many who were paralyzed and lame were healed.
And there was great joy in that city. "
Acts 8 / 4 – 8

WOW - what a dimension of God and therefore also for HIS people! TODAY!

Imagine that for a moment!
Crippled people – bones crunch and crack when they straighten and come back into place in front of you.

Amputated limbs grow back - in front of the eyes of those present, who almost faint.

Incurable diseases - simply disappear in the name of Jesus, taking all the effects and restrictions with them.

Psychoses, schizophrenia, mental illnesses are suddenly no longer there because the name of Jesus has eliminated them.

Addicts are visibly and tangibly freed from alcohol, drugs, sex addiction, paedophilia, gambling addiction and other addictions and the physical, emotional and psychological signs of decay are healed immediately in front of everyone's eyes.

Look this up in the Bible, in the Gospel of Mark 5.
A totally blatant story. Pure nightmare. A horror experience for disciples. Not for beginners or the faint-hearted.
A completely crazy guy, untameable, demonically strong, all chains broken, living in a burial cave in the cemetery, raving

57

and raving like a madman (which he was) → he meets Jesus and the power of the Holy Spirit and is immediately free, healthy and completely clear in the head and Jesus simply sends him home, without rehab, supervision or aftercare.

In contrast, Alfred Hitchcock or Klaus Kinski with their horror films or novels are "Good night stories" for children

And now imagine that this happens on a massive scale in German, English or other psychiatric centres in all countries. That makes headlines worldwide. It reduces healthcare costs. The health minister freaks out with joy.

The health insurance companies would be happy to pay their 'tithe' to the respective municipalities. ☺

And much more, the list of possibilities is endless ... and that is what the Word of God says.

Jesus would have a social impact if HE were allowed to. And we as churches would receive many medals and honours because we do so many good and "impossible" things for the nations and the afflicted people in the name of Jesus.

Hope for the land

We live in Germany, a Christian country (and it will remain so!), a good and blessed country, the country of the Reformation, where Luther denounced and broke through the religious curse of idolatry, distortion of the Word of God, occultism and spiritualism, massive worship of saints and human beings, abuse of power and profiteering, forgiveness of sins through money payments and much more, in order to re-establish the centre of the Gospel and the Word of God, namely:

**Salvation only by God's grace
and Justification by Jesus Christ alone**

Back to the roots, back to the beginning, reset, new start - that was the message. He had a full revelation through the Holy Spirit in the midst of this religious jungle.

To bring people back into the arms of God by personally accepting what Jesus did on the cross for me, for you, for all people.
Jesus paid the price for redemption, winning an everlasting victory over the devil, death, sin and sickness so that we can be reconciled with God again.

*"Blessed is the nation whose God is the LORD,
The people He has chosen as His own inheritance."*
Psalms 33 / 12

*"Ask of Me, and I will give You
The nations for Your inheritance,
And the ends of the earth for Your possession."*
Psalms 2 / 8

Germany is part of the inheritance that Jesus asked the Father for. And that applies to every country on earth. YOUR country as well! Jesus has purchased a worldwide redemption. The nations belong to HIM. HE paid for Germany, (England, USA, etc.) Germany and the others belong to JESUS, no matter if other people disagree, redemption is available, it just needs to be accepted. Hallelujah!

I am writing here specifically for Germany, but the same applies to your country.

We would do well as a people, as a nation, to bring the God of the Bible back into our minds and make HIM our Lord again.
Actually, we in Germany and our politicians, regardless of party colour, are obliged to do so by our constitution!
(So here's a little digression into our German legal foundations - as I understand it).

This would mean that we, as a present-day society, would be doing what we gave ourselves as a German nation on 23 May 1949 in the Constitution!

Basic Law for the Federal Republic of Germany Preamble

Conscious of his responsibility before God and mankind, Inspired by the will to serve the peace of the world as an equal member of a united Europe, the German people have adopted this Basic Law by virtue of their constituent power. The Germans in the federal states of Baden-Württemberg, Bayern, Berlin, Brandenburg, Bremen, Hamburg, Hessen, Mecklenburg-Vorpommern, Niedersachsen, Nordrhein-Westfalen, Rheinland-Pfalz, Saarland, Sachsen, Sachsen-Anhalt, Schleswig-Holstein and Thüringen have, in free self-determination, completed the unity and freedom of Germany.

This Basic Law thus applies to the entire German people.
(text source: Internet / Bundesministerium der Justiz / www.gesetze-im-internet.de, / 27.04.2024)

Wow! That's really strong. It applies to the entire German people and everyone who lives in Germany. Not just German citizens.
But they don't talk about that much anymore.
But hold on tight, it gets even better and clearer!

Constitution of the Free State of Bavaria from 08.12.1946 in the version published on 15. December 1998 Preamble

In view of the ruins to which a state and social order without God, without conscience and without respect for human dignity has led the survivors of the Second World War, In the firm resolve to permanently secure the blessings of peace, humanity and justice for future German generations, the Bavarian people, mindful of its more than one thousand years of history, hereby adopt the following democratic constitution
(text source: Internet, www.gesetze-bayern.de, 29.04.2024)

The preamble is not yet a detailed law, but it lays the foundation, the cornerstone, the standard for all subsequent laws. It is like the spiritual background to the constitution or basic law.

WIKIPEDIA (29.04.2024):
Preamble (from Latin praeambulare "to precede"; via Middle Latin praeambulum "introduction") today refers to a usually solemn declaration written in elevated language at the beginning of a document, in particular a constitution or an international treaty. For example, the German Basic

Law, the Federal Constitution of the Swiss Confederation and the Austrian State Treaty (1955) contain a preamble. Nowadays, they serve to describe the motives, intentions and purposes of their authors and reflect the respective basic consensus. In times of work on a European constitution, the mention of a special religious reference or an invocatio dei in the preamble is controversial.

The Basic Law is superior to the state constitutions.

It is significant, intentional and explicitly mentioned that this preamble of the Basic Law (with the responsibility before God ...) also applies to the federal states, which have not anchored a reference to God in their state constitutions.

A look at the constitutions of the 17 German federal states provides an interesting picture of the so-called "reference to God".

Not all federal states have included it in the preamble to their constitutions.

Without reference to God:
Berlin, Saarland, Sachsen, Sachsen-Anhalt, Hessen, Schleswig-Holstein, Mecklenburg-Vorpommern, Hamburg, Bremen, Thüringen, Brandenburg,

With reference to God:
Bayern, Baden-Württemberg, Niedersachsen, Rheinland-Pfalz
(Hallelujah!)

One federal state defines it even more precisely by recognising, even defining, **the God of the Bible as the source of law and the creator of all human community.**
WOW – Hallelujah – Suuuuper – Yippie – Congratulations - thank God!
Germany is not lost yet!

Constitution of Rheinland-Pfalz, from 18.05.1947: Preamble:

Conscious of our responsibility before God, the source of law and creator of all human community, ...
(text source: Internet / aktuelle Onlineversionen der Länderverfassungen / 2024)

But let's stick with the Bavarians.
Because I live here, because I love it and because Jesus loves it. (the other federal states too, of course ☺)
So we're not talking about the footballers from FC Bayern Munich, but about the people of Bavaria in general, the Free State of Bavaria and the Bavarian constitution.

Let's also take a quick look at the school's educational mandate in the Bavarian Constitution, where it is emphasised again and gets to the point.

Article 131, paragraph 2 of the Bavarian Constitution

(2) The highest educational goals are reverence for God, Respect for religious conviction and for human dignity, self-control, a sense of responsibility and willingness to take responsibility, helpfulness, open-mindedness for all that is true, good and beautiful, and a sense of responsibility for nature and the environment.

What an educational goal!
The "old people" knew it!

It goes without saying that the authors of the Basic Law and the corresponding state constitutions speak of the God of the Bible. Shortly after the end of the Second World War, there were no "other, imported gods" in Germany. There was no spread of beliefs in Allah, Buddha or other powers. On a small scale perhaps, but without any social impact. That only came much later.

It was the conviction in the God of the Bible, in Jesus the Saviour and the Holy Spirit as God-given helper that had grown, lived and experienced over many centuries. The relevant public holidays speak for themselves. Christmas, Easter, Ascension Day, Pentecost.
It is clearly about God, the Father of Jesus Christ and the Holy Spirit. And about no one else.

It was a "simple" faith in the God of the Bible, of course and unfortunately also with all its lived errors and misunderstandings, abuses and theological misinterpretations. But also with the majority of the blessings that emanated from this faith in God.
But the reason and the general direction was the God of the Bible and HE still is today.

In my opinion and conviction, the God of the Bible, the Father of the Saviour Jesus Christ, is still the sole foundation in the country according to the Basic Law and some state constitutions.

And that with all tolerance towards people from all over the world who believe something different and live according to it. They may and should do so, it is their right, but it is not the basis of our Basic Law. And that is why Islam, or whatever else, does not belong to Germany. Sorry - it's not in the Basic Law.

The much-cited absolute separation of church and state does not exist in this form; it is a "partnership", regulated by a large number of treaties and agreements. Right now, as of August 2024, it is once again a political issue to finally disentangle and end these treaties.

The state as an "institution", as an "organ of state" has given itself the NEUTRALITY COMMANDMENT, i.e. it must and wants to make it possible for everyone to have and practise religious freedom.

But ultimately it does not change the preamble with the reference to God.
As I said, this is my conviction and point of view, anyone who sees it differently, sees it differently.
THANK GOD we have this freedom in Germany.

But with all the confusion, forgetting and softening, we need a fresh revelation about this God of the Bible, HIS loving plans for our country and people, to recognise HIS calling for Germany and to get involved.

> *„Where there is no revelation,*
> *the people cast off restraint;*
> *But happy is he who keeps the law. "*
> (for us today it is the Word of God - the Bible)
> Proverbs 29 / 18

Imagine an apostle or prophet is a permanent member of the "Deutscher Bundestag" (= the government) and passes on prophetic words of God, warnings and ideas of God and he is heard!
Daydream? Crazy? Or an answer to prayer?
Let's take a look.

Incidentally, there are biblical examples of this.
Take a look at the prophets in the Old Testament
(e.g. 2 Kings 6)
or in the New Testament, what men and women of God said directly to the kings and rulers.

Have fun and gain knowledge while searching. ☺

Why don't you write down what you understand by miracle or what you would categorise as a miracle?
Try your own definition.
Have fun - I think the list will be long!

Situation in the land

I don't think we need to develop this thematically here, everyone in the country sees, hears and experiences it in many different ways.
We are currently living in a sea of hopelessness, a lack of future prospects, fears, insecurities, helplessness, outrageous arrogance and great godlessness.

You watch the news and then you actually need a counsellor, psychiatrist or other good trauma therapist. Some people also take alcohol or drugs.
It's a horror show! Just murder and manslaughter, war, violence, crime, lies, greed, selfishness and so much more.

Where is the news about the God of miracles, his help, messages of hope, salvation and prospects? Where do we still hear or read about it?

Of course, these are initially the main attributes of the messages of Jesus' church, the Bible and not the news. But we should provide them with the material they share.
The stuff that people's dreams are made of.
It should become known in the country.
Jesus showed these miracles, and all of Israel spoke about them. Supporters and opponents.
The first church showed it and lived it and the whole world talked about it and was shaken up and changed.
Don't you believe it? Have a look!

„ But when they did not find them, (Paul and others)
they dragged Jason and some brethren
to the rulers of the city, crying out,
These who have turned the world upside down
have come here too. "
Acts 17 / 6

The message of Jesus had reached many countries in the then known world. Even in Greece. And in Thessalonica, the religious leaders hated the apostle Paul, persecuted him ☹ † and wanted to lynch him. But they didn't succeed! ☺

But what do we look like today? What has been lost to us?

As already mentioned, even on many websites of churches and free churches there is no reference to the **"miraculous"** actions of Jesus. Zero - nothing! What a pity.
Although it is clearly part of the church programme, or should be. And it should be proclaimed in every conceivable way.
The old King David already knew and did this:

„From David.
Bless the LORD, O my soul;
And all that is within me, bless His holy name!
Bless the LORD, O my soul,
And forget not all His benefits:
Who forgives all your iniquities,
Who heals all your diseases,
Who redeems your life from destruction,
Who crowns you with lovingkindness and tender mercies,
Who satisfies your mouth with good things,
So that your youth is renewed like the eagle's.“
Psalms 103 / 1 - 5

„I will praise You, O LORD, with my whole heart;
I will tell of all Your marvelous works.
I will be glad and rejoice in You;
I will sing praise to Your name, O Most High.“
Psalm 9 / 1 + 2

*„ Many, O L*ORD *my God, are Your wonderful works*
Which You have done;
And Your thoughts toward us
Cannot be recounted to You in order;
If I would declare and speak of them,
They are more than can be numbered. "
Psalm 40 / 5

„ We will not hide them from their children,
*Telling to the generation to come the praises of the L*ORD,
And His strength and His wonderful works
that He has done. "
Psalm 78 / 4

Even in many sermons of the large churches and other congregations, especially on high holidays, when the churches are usually full and enjoy media attention, more is preached about politics, the environment and climate, saving frogs, against certain parties, etc. Instead of Jesus, the only way to God and salvation.
God is the salvation, the solution and the way - in Jesus Christ. Not the parties. They won't take us to paradise, rather the opposite.

Jesus as Saviour and Redeemer is often no longer the focus. People's repentance and conversion, the necessity of a personal relationship with Jesus, the freedom, peace, healing and liberation experienced through Jesus are simply watered down, softened or even completely ignored.
Some sermons give the impression that a new political party has emerged.
The "Church Party".
But unfortunately there is often so little JESUS in the programme.

But that was and is not the message of Jesus.

He did not die for climate change, frog migration or animal welfare.

It is also important that we take care of that, but first it is about our personal salvation through Jesus.

„For what profit is it to a man
if he gains the whole world, and loses his own soul?
Or what will a man give in exchange for his soul?"
Matthew 16 / 26

Jesus died for the " welfare of mankind" , that is, for the forgiveness of sin, salvation, eternal life with God, deliverance from sin and from the bondage of the devil and much more.

„ for the Son of Man (Jesus) *has come*
to seek and to save that which was lost."
Luke 19 / 10

„how God anointed Jesus of Nazareth with the Holy Spirit
and with power, who went about doing good and healing all
who were oppressed by the devil,
(who were under the dominion/influence of the devil)
for God was with Him."
Acts 10 / 38

This is for us! This is our chance!
Jesus is looking for us to save us!
Yippee!

I don't want to appear unfair here or pretend that everything is bad.

NO - not at all! We have many serious and fiery followers of Jesus, many good churches in the country that proclaim the gospel with a clear edge, fearlessly, without pious fabric softener and mainstream spirit.

THANK GOD - there are churches in the country that have clear, biblical teaching and preaching and many reports of miracles through the intervention of God.

Congratulations - heroes of God!
Thank you for every testimony of the work of Jesus on your websites, social media and other opportunities. Keep it up! Even more! It's getting through!
People register it and get hope.
Our country must hear it.

And that gives us hope for more.
Hope for our country.
Hope for our churches.
Hope for you.
Hope for me.

Thank you Jesus!

Jesus shows us HIS Father, the God of the Bible, as a God of miracles, of supernatural events and interventions, of hope, far beyond our thinking.

If we rob Him of HIS miracles and power, of the intention of HIS supernatural help, then we create a completely false image of God.

Then we no longer believe in the God of the Bible, the Father of Jesus Christ and in the work of the Holy Spirit, who comes with DYNAMIS, but in any god, as there were and are millions of them in the cultures of this world.

And we wonder why people don't recognise Jesus as the Son of God and don't want to know anything about HIM. This is "no wonder"! ☹

Christians are people who believe in Jesus Christ, who have consciously entrusted their lives to HIM, who live with HIM every day, who talk to HIM, who love, heed and try to do His word. They should know and experience this powerful dimension of the miracle-working God of the Bible and pass it on and show it as a message of hope.

The world is waiting for the church of Jesus to rise ...

*„ **You are the salt of the earth;***
but if the salt loses its flavour, how shall it be seasoned?
It is then good for nothing
but to be thrown out and trampled underfoot by men.
You are the light of the world.
A city that is set on a hill cannot be hidden.
Nor do they light a lamp and put it under a basket,
but on a lampstand, and it gives light to all
who are in the house.
Let your light so shine before men,
that they may see your good works
and glorify your Father in heaven. "
Matthew 5 / 13 - 16

„ Then the men of the city (Jericho)
said to Elisha, (the prophet)
Please notice, the situation of this city is pleasant,
as my lord sees; but the water is bad,
and the ground barren. "
And he said, Bring me a new bowl, and put salt in it.
So they brought it to him.
Then he went out to the source of the water, ...

... and cast in the salt there, and said,
Thus says the LORD: I have healed this water;
from it there shall be no more death or barrenness.
So the water remains healed to this day,
according to the word of Elisha which he spoke."
2 Kings 2 / 19 – 22

„Declare His glory among the nations,
His wonders among all peoples."
Psalm 96 / 3

Even today, the followers of Jesus are still light and salt in a lost, hopeless and corrupt world.

God wants to throw "his salt" into these evil, dead, sterile, barren springs so that they become healthy.

God has not changed, HE still wants to do it, people, governments and nations should see and experience His love, power, help and infinite possibilities.

HIS power and miracles for a world that desperately needs it. Germany and the nations are not yet completely lost.

There is hope for your country!

The following reports are intended to encourage you to experience this "WONDER - ful" God in your own life.

You and I are not indifferent to God. HE wants to and can help. In HIS way.

Let yourself be surprised!

When we talk about miracles we have experienced, we are always asked whether what we have experienced really happened and are now writing down here in part.

YES - we're not lying to you. We would never dare to do that. It all happened like this. Honestly. Our word on it! Even if it sometimes sounds "unbelievable".
And there are often witnesses to this.

Travelling with Jesus

Ever since Andra and I got married, we have loved travelling. Foreign countries and cultures, getting to know people, their customs, food (! ☺) and everything that goes with it. We have travelled to many countries, initially just as normal tourists, then more and more to churches to get to know them, learn from them, serve them and experience Jesus together.

In November 2001, we were invited to a large pastors' conference in La Plata, Argentina. We were excited and enthusiastic, full of expectation.
It was one of our first major trips in the ministry of Jesus and the church there had taken over the planning.

When we arrived, it hit us like a shock!
Accommodation in a leisure camp with simple little sleeping houses. And a strict separation of the sexes. Even married couples! We hadn't realised that and so our suitcases were not packed "gender-segregated". Everything was mixed.

The men in a small house, I think we were 8 (!) in bunk beds, a small window approx. 50 x 50 cm, with an estimated daytime temperature of 35 degrees and a night-time temperature of 25 degrees and millions of mosquitoes just waiting to suck "German blood" again at night. So practically going to the "foreigner" for dinner or to the "German pub".
Good night and cheers - meal time!

And the best thing was that late in the evening, after all the activities had finished, the Argentinian male staff came into our room - there were 4 or 5 of them - and simply lay down on the floor between the bunk beds with blankets.
If you had to go to the toilet at night, there was a risk of hurting someone on the floor by stepping on them.

When we asked them why they were doing this, they told us that they wanted to be with us. Well - that's another way of looking at it. Didn't make sense to us, but it made them happy. Just being around the "German pastors" - that was an honour for them.

It was similar for the women, 5 or 6 together, with a small bathroom with toilet. You can imagine what was going on there. Especially in the morning, each with her own beauty time.
Mamma Mia.

For the local church it was an upmarket leisure centre, for us it was rather primitive.

But we felt the love and care of the Argentinian brothers and sisters for us German pastors and leaders, and that made us endure the whole thing. It cost them a lot of money and effort to accommodate and care for us there.
Once again in retrospect: Thank you very much for your love for us!

So we swallowed all our disappointment, reminded ourselves to be humble and not arrogant and to trust in Jesus that HE has the best for us.
(even if it sometimes doesn't look like it ☺)

„And we know that all things work together for good
to those who love God,
to those who are the called according to His purpose."
Romans 8 / 28

the German translation here says that everything must serve for the "BEST", not only for the "GOOD"
And the addressee is us! We love God!
So it was the "BEST" thing for us at the moment. Even if I

didn't really understand it. But God checks it - for me, for us. Trust is the order of the day.

It was a wonderful conference, powerful encounters with men and women of God, friendships instigated by God that continue to this day. We learnt about a previously unknown power of the Holy Spirit that changed our lives and those of our church forever.
It was God's plan that we should be there, HE wanted to bring us into a new dimension of faith. And HE did that too!

The friendship and ministry with Apostle Raul Reyes and his wife Betty, which began then and still continues today, is just one of the blessings that God gave us as the "BEST" there in Argentina, despite simple accommodation, mosquitoes, etc.
Thank you Jesus!

We stayed in Argentina for a while after the conference to get to know some of the country and recover from the stresses and strains of the overnight camp. It had been a bit of a pain in the bum and we had a bit of a quarrel with God because it didn't live up to our expectations in terms of accommodation and comfort. I don't want to go into details here, that would be unfair.
But we already told Jesus that.

Our initial plan was to fly to the famous waterfalls in Iguazú in the north of the country. It was supposed to be beautiful (!) there.

So we bought two flight tickets, economy class, and off we went to the airport.
Check-in → Boarding passes Economy - Class → Waiting → Finally boarding.

A stewardess stood at the boarding door of the aircraft and checked our boarding passes once again.

"Ah - row 1, seats A + B", so we went through the small First Class (it had three rows, then a curtain separating it from Economy Class) and wanted to sit in the first row of Economy Class. She came after us and repeated that we had row 1.

Our Spanish was anything but useful, but we pointed to our seats in the first row, showed our boarding passes again and said "Economy class, row 1".

The stewardess nodded in a friendly manner and pointed clearly and firmly to row 1 in First Class. "Row 1 - there! Come with me!"

We briefly discussed "economy class" and "first class" because we thought she must have confused us, as we had only bought and paid for the basic class. We finally gave up, she was the boss in the ring and very friendly, very persistent and very determined.

So we resigned ourselves to our fate in First Class. Some things you just have to put up with.

Thick, soft and wide leather seats, only two seats to the right and left of the centre aisle in each row, instead of the usual three.

Our stewardess came back and offered us two glasses of champagne to welcome us and told us that she was responsible for the four passengers in row 1 and that two other stewardesses were responsible for the other two rows. (There was no sign of a shortage of staff at the time)

Hey Buddy - I'm telling you! We were spoilt rotten. Snacks, coffee, espresso, hot food. Everything your heart desired and as much as you wanted.

I prayed to Jesus, "Lord - never let this flight come to an end"!

Unfortunately, my prayer was not answered!

And suddenly we felt it was a compensation from God for us, a "cream - candy", a super comfort - plaster for the camp. HE was now giving us a gift.
We enjoooooooy it!

Jesus had "up - graded" us

And then the hot meal was served.
Mamma Mia!

On porcelain plates with the right cutlery. Sharp knives. Not plastic rubbish.

Argentinian Angus Steak, medium+, a huge rag of meat, tender as butter, perfect.
The heavens had opened up a little further for me.
Hallelujah! Thank you Jesus for the Argentinian Angus cattle. We received them (at least a piece of them) with full thanksgiving.

> *„For every creature of God is good,*
> *and nothing is to be refused*
> *if it is received with thanksgiving;*
> *for it is sanctified by the word of God and prayer."*
> 1 Timothy 4 / 4 + 5

Were Angus cattle created by God? → Yes! → check!
Is it reprehensible? → No! → check!
Did we take it with thanksgiving? → but so yeees! → check!
Sanctified by the Word of God and our prayer? → Yes, amen!
Thank you God! → check!
All checks positive. All successful. All good! Everything is fine! TAKE THE STEAK!

It was like heaven on earth - aah – wait, not quite, we were in the air. Between heaven and earth, so to speak. So actually a lot closer to heaven anyway.

(Remember: ... all things for the BEST ...)

As I write this now, my mouth is still watering at the memory, or is it again?

After about 2 ½ hours of flying (I repeat: unfortunately my prayer was not answered), we arrived back on the ground. The harsh reality had us again, at around 45 degrees in the shadow. Iguazú airport.

Welcome! Willkommen! Bienvenido!

At the exit from the airport there were small offices where you could buy vouchers for hotel rooms.

We went into an office, got some information and then bought a voucher for a small, simple double room with breakfast for 3 days. It was pretty cheap.

We didn't have any great expectations, it had to be clean and have a reasonably wide bed.

And then we took a taxi to the hotel and went to reception with our voucher. The hotel didn't look too bad. Thank you Jesus!

Not a backyard flophouse.

"A double room with breakfast, 3 nights, already reserved and paid for by the office at the airport"!

We presented our voucher in a cosmopolitan manner.

"Yes, the man from the airport office has already called and announced you"

The man at reception turned round, took a room key from the wall and told us to follow him, he would show us the room.

We were a bit nervous about what to expect.

He walked along the long corridor on the ground floor and

stopped at the end to unlock a door to a room.

"Oh dear" we thought, at the end of the corridor are normally the broom cupboards. Let's see what the guy from the airport office had sold us. It was a reservation into the unknown. So it was practically the proverbial "pig in a poke".

But we had prayed beforehand that we would not be tricked and that we would have a good stay.

Above the door it said "Honeymoon Suite", probably sarcastically referring to the expected broom cupboard.

And the door opened ...
... **AND THE WINNER IS ... Tadaa! → US!**

We were in a huge suite, a super-large bed (which belongs to Honeymoon! So to put it mildly and in a "youth - free" way), the glass front of the room looked out onto a marvellous, subtropical garden with direct access to the pool. Everything at its best.
We were gobsmacked, overwhelmed and in disbelief.

"There must be a mistake" I said to the hotel employee. "We have booked a simple double room with breakfast, not the wedding suite"

"No, you have booked this suite with full board".

"No, double room with breakfast". I just saw my VISA card disappear into the abyss and, as an old policeman, I could already see us getting caught up in fraud and the Argentinian mafia.
"No - No", the discussion went back and forth.
We refused to believe what we were seeing.

But we had prayed. That's what you normally do as a

Christian - or at least that's what you should do.

But we often limit ourselves in prayer because our expectations and faith are in the wrong direction or are too small or we don't even believe what we are praying for. We pray because we pray.

And we heard the Holy Spirit quietly saying within us "trust me" and "...all things for the BEST, who love God" and "no mafia".

So, to be on the safe side, we went back to reception to check the booking. Honest as we are, we showed our voucher again, which had everything on it, including the price we had paid.

"Yes, that's right. Everything is correct," the man told us kindly. So somehow he must have seen other vouchers.

He showed us his reservation book, where it was written in black and white:
- − Honeymoon Suite,
- − three nights with full board,
- − for Günther and Andra Kunstmann, Alemania, ...
- − ... and ALREADY PAID!

We couldn't really believe it. God had "up-graded" us again. Just like that. Without us having prayed for it or begged at the hotel.
God is so good!

No idea how HE always does it. Boarding system, airline accounting (they certainly have no financial loss either) hotel reservation system etc.

?????

HE is simply GOD, the one with unlimited possibilities.

From economy to first class, from a simple, small double room to a spacious suite with direct access to a small paradise with pool.

From a simple breakfast to full board. Man - I tell you, the great tables were bending under the fantastic food. God is so good!

HE knew exactly how to give us great joy. After the "hardships and disappointment". Just like that.
Because HE simply enjoys doing something good for his children.
This is one of HIS traits that HE wants to show much more often in your and my life.
HE is the perfect provider, the perfect ""caretaker"", the giver of gifts, just as a father simply gives gifts to his children without anything in return and rejoices in their joyful reaction.

„But without faith it is impossible to please Him,
for he who comes to God must believe that He is,
*and that He is a **rewarder***
of those who diligently seek Him."
Hebrews 11 / 6

„Now to Him who
is able to do exceedingly abundantly
above all that we ask or think,
according to the power that works in us,
to Him be glory in the church by Christ Jesus
to all generations, forever and ever. Amen."
Ephesians 3 / 20 + 21

„Look at the birds of the air,
for they neither sow nor reap nor gather into barns;
yet your heavenly Father feeds them.
Are you not of more value than they?"
Matthew 6 / 26

„So why do you worry about clothing?
Consider the lilies of the field, how they grow:
they neither toil nor spin;
and yet I say to you that even Solomon in all his glory
was not arrayed like one of these.
Now if God so clothes the grass of the field,
which today is, and tomorrow is thrown into the oven,
will He not much more clothe you,
O you of little faith?
Therefore do not worry, saying,
What shall we eat? 'or What shall we drink?
or What shall we wear?
For after all these things the Gentiles seek.
For your heavenly Father knows
that you need all these things.
But seek first the kingdom of God and His righteousness,
and all these things shall be added to you.*"*
Matthew 6 / 28 – 33

„as His divine power has given to us
all things that pertain to life and godliness,
through the knowledge of Him
who called us by glory and virtue,"
2 Peter 1 / 3

If these are not promises. Clear announcements from the " Caretaker", from the Provider, from the Rewarder, from our Lord Jesus!
Trust him. An "upgrade" is waiting.

And here we are, at the reception, overwhelmed, disbelieving, joyfully confused, excited as we were back then at our wedding altar.

(of course - it was the Honeymoon Suite ☺)

We, the pastors from Germany, travelling with Jesus since our youth, oil-soaked and waterproof, motivating and leading others to faith and we realised:

We are people of little faith!

Just like Jesus said a little further up.
To us.
Mamma Mia!

What an embarrassment for both of us "heroes of faith"!

But STOP!
Jesus will never embarrass us, but will point us to things of faith, open the door to the next level of learning so that we can progress further than before, experience Him more than before, gain more victories than before, ... but not embarrass us.

And the Holy Spirit spoke to us and explained to us the thought patterns in which we are usually stuck.

We live here in the world and under its influences. We are characterised by slogans that we sometimes even say ourselves.

Nothing without money

Nothing comes from nothing

You have to perform

What costs nothing is worth nothing

You have to prove yourself

Self-realisation

and a few more words of "wisdom".

And Jesus goes exactly the opposite way.
With God it's not about performance, not about "you have to, so that ...", we cannot earn, buy, beg or blackmail our way to God's pleasure, favour, love, blessing, forgiveness and eternal life,
→ but only let us GIVE.

We worry about things that destroy us slowly and leave us sleepless, and God already has a solution.

We plan our lives frantically and God wants to draw my attention to HIS plans for my life.

God wants to slow us down, bring us to rest, guide us with HIS peace and word and sometimes we make life so difficult for ourselves. The hamster wheel is spinning faster and faster. The way is the goal - says the hamster and falls off his beloved turbo wheel with a heart attack after a new daily best time. On the way, but no destination reached, just actions.
He thought he was on his way. Action, enough sweating.
Too bad, life had fooled him.

Clothes, future, bank account, job, leisure activities, finding a partner, friends, family, commitment and and and and ... and!
☹ †
Was that all?

The Holy Spirit taught us that we should also look more to the FATHER as our provider, and that without return.

We should focus more on the dimension of the Kingdom of God, even now here on earth.
As a child of God, I am part of this "supernatural dimension, the kingdom of God". I already belong to it. Spiritually speaking, I am already there.

„He has delivered us from the power of darkness
and conveyed us into the kingdom of the Son of His love,
in whom we have redemption through His blood,
the forgiveness of sins."
Colossians 1 / 13 + 14

Of course, this does not mean that we should go through life without a plan, irresponsibly, naively or " blue-eyed", not caring about anything, well - God will take care of it.

NO - that's not what Jesus means.
But we should get rid of the tormenting worries and thoughts and not let them control us.

And give God, the Father, the opportunity to simply give us gifts more often.

"Oh, but we didn't need that now" or "that wouldn't have been necessary, I can't even accept that!" do we recognise that?

And God thinks to himself: "Oh, I could do that more often, because it's needed."

Many of us have somehow forgotten how to allow ourselves to be given gifts unconditionally. Just like that - without a gift in return. We always think we are obliged to give back the same value. It's no longer a gift, it's a business.

When God gives us gifts or wants to give us gifts, we often cannot believe it when it happens, even though it is written 1000 times in the Bible.
We are told some amazing things there.

We don't expect it at all.
Our mind is at odds with itself. It's not our learned, trained thought pattern. Our plausibility check does not allow it. The world has left its mark on us. The logic, the experiences in this world.

"The plausibility check, also known as a plausibility control, plausibility test or plausibilisation, is a method in which a value or generally a result is roughly checked to see whether or not it can be plausible, i.e. acceptable, plausible or comprehensible."
(Text source: www.deutsches-ausschreibungsblatt.de, 09.05.2024)

I found this explanation fitting.

Then we start discussing, it can't be what I can't check, our logic has us firmly in its grip.

Many people do this, unfortunately we do it again and again.

Logic is generally used
to describe rational reasoning and,
in particular, its theory -
the theory of reasoning or
theory of thought.
In logic, the structure of arguments is
analysed with regard to their validity,
regardless of the content of the statements
Wikipedia, 31.08.2024

And we usually get stuck in it. It comes up automatically. Learned, instilled, trained.

"Hi Günther - it's me again - your logic!"

I can only free myself from this grip with a conscious effort in order to see and dare to do something different.

That's why the Word of God has a great command for us to break through this.

„And do not be conformed to this world,
but be transformed by the renewing of your mind,
that you may prove
what is that good and acceptable and perfect will of God."
Romans 12 / 2

That is the secret. The access to this thinking.

"The renewing of our mind"

Obviously this is necessary. If something needs to be replaced, then something is no longer fully functional, otherwise there would be no need to renew it.

Or the circumstances have changed and now you have to correct, readjust, replace something, enable new functions, download updates.

We need this renewing together with the Holy Spirit and the Word of God, so that …

"we can prove what God's will is"

And HIS will is, among other things, to give us gifts.

HE is a giving God.

Aha! Now it rings a bell, now the penny drops, now a light dawns on me! Whole chandeliers!

Without this renewing we don't even realise it. We're stuck in the old. Our brains won't allow anything else. What a rascal!

We should develop a heavenly thought pattern, train ourselves in spiritual principles and learn to have spiritual, supernatural experiences.
And then we become "travellers between the worlds". We live here on earth with all the natural things, but also through faith in the heavenly world with its principles and possibilities.
The Bible is full of it, Jesus showed it, as did the first church.
So what are you waiting for? Let's go - let's do it!

Remember the first report here in the book about the little boy's eye healing. What was the mother's reaction to his announcement that he could see something in his blind eye?

"NO - you can't. The eye is blind"
"Yes I can!" → "No" → "Yes!" → "No" → "Yes!"

The plausibility check jumps in and rejects it. Logically, empirically correct, it has always been like this - and yet it is often wrong. But at some point (hopefully as quickly as possible) it dawns on the believer: "Should God have a hand in this?"

Then we suddenly take a different approach. We can suddenly accept it or at least consider it. Some full braking of our hamster wheel is perhaps an "emergency braking" initiated by Jesus?

"Row 1, seats A + B" remember?
"First class, sit down please" → "NO - we have economy class" .
"No" → "Yes!" → "No" → "Yes, you do!" → "No"

"Honeymoon Suite" → "No, simple double room"
"No" → "Yes!" → "No" → "Yes, you do!" → "No"

Man or man, how long does it take for the penny to drop? Do you feel the same way?

The plausibility check can also annoy me, block me and hinder the blessing, the gift of God. Because I simply don't allow it. Unconsciously cannot allow it. I find it so difficult to simply allow myself to be blessed.

And sometimes this control is also good, a protection, a blessing.
And that is precisely the problem, we have to differentiate, check.

After this small (or big?) lesson from the Holy Spirit, we once again surrendered to the wonderful, warm and giving hand of God and enjoyed our time in the suite we had been given and the additional full board. It was heavenly! (or almost)

20 years after our honeymoon, once again a gift of time in the Honeymoon Suite, the second honeymoon, a gift from our Father in heaven.
How brilliant is that!

And because this lesson is hard to learn and yet keeps knocking on our door, here's another small example.

We were at the end of our multi-week preaching and healing trip in Brazil. The last evening, powerful healings took place, people were saved - it was a heavenly atmosphere and power.

We went to the pastor's house after the service and our Brazilian friend and driver, Robson, was with us.

We still needed a domestic flight from Rio de Janeiro to Sao Paulo for the next day.

Thank God for the internet - so flight searched - found - booked → proceed to pay.
No problem, we have VISA.
So the data entered, everything correct - ENTER pressed and delighted that everything works so smoothly with modern methods. The world's system also works without faith and Jesus.

"AS IF" - I hadn't reckoned with "verified by VISA". A security function that actually makes sense.
You have to go to your VISA website and enter the PIN they send to your mobile phone number to verify and authorise the payment.

And that was the problem.

The deposited number was German, didn't work in Brazil at the time, no verification, no release, no ticket, no flight. ☹

"The booking process was cancelled" was the dry note on the PC.
A slight panic crept up our spines. "But that can't be right now. Lord - help!"
(Aah – so now after all)

Our friend rang the airline and asked. Yes, the booking attempt was traceable, cancelled because no payment was made. The process was closed.

"Can we make a reservation by phone, we'll pay at the flight counter tomorrow, that's fine."
"No - we can't accept reservations over the phone. Come directly to the flight counter at the airport tomorrow and start

the ticket purchase process all over again!"

Excellent. Stay calm, we had prayed.

So the next day, our friend drove us to the airport very early because we didn't know how long it would take us. We went straight to the airline counter where we had tried to buy a ticket the night before.

A lady, a friendly employee took care of our request. We explained to her the failed purchase attempt from the last evening and that she should please check whether the two seats on the special flight were still available at the favourable price.

"Yes - here they are. Everything you were looking for yesterday is still available now"
"Thank you Jesus!" A stone fell from our hearts.

"We would like to buy two tickets at these conditions. Can we pay with VISA? Without verification?"

"Yes - no problem. Please give me your passports for personal details."
("Lord - that works! Great, thank you!")
"Here, please, our two passports."

The lady took my passport first, typed the surname into the system and wanted to continue with the first name.
"Wait a second! The system tells me that you already have a reservation for these two tickets."

"NO! We don't have a reservation. It was not possible. We even phoned to enquire."
"YES! - you have a reservation."
"No" → "Yes" → "No" → Yes!!!!! The system is not wrong. I have two reservations here for Günther and Andra"

OK - apparently the system had taken over and saved our data after all. It can happen, the computer can do other things than what it says, it's only "a stupid human".

"But I couldn't pay last night, I want to do it now" I pulled out my VISA and put it on the counter.
"Yes - ok, we'll do that in a second. She took the VISA and continued with the reservation process.

"Oh - I see here that the two tickets are already paid for! She gave me back the VISA.

The interested and watchful reader can already guess what happened next!
So how?

"No" → "Yes" → "No" → Yes!!!!! The system is not wrong. The tickets are paid for."

We were once again confused, amazed and surprised.
We hadn't realised it again.
God was in control.

She printed everything out for us, wished us a good flight, turned round and left us standing alone and perplexed.

We left baffled and the flight went smoothly.

"The online booking probably worked after all, we'll see when we get home with the VISA account."
(we just can't stop - can you see it?)

A relative, who is also a Christian, was completely convinced that it was simply a computer problem. Nothing to do with God and faith.
There are more Christians who don't get it ☹ !

The two flights were NEVER debited.
God had given them to us as a gift.
How HE did that remains his secret.
When we are with HIM one day in eternity, I will ask him.
That interests me. Honestly.

Our friend, Apostle Raul from Argentina, told us something similar about supply miracles.
Several members of his church had experienced it independently of each other.

They had gone to the cash machine to withdraw their last pesos.
"100 pesos" → enter PIN → money chute opens → thousands of pesos come out.
The people, honest as they are because they live with Jesus, go to the bank to give the money back.
The bank employee checks everything in the computer system and says that everything is ok, the booking is correct and the money is theirs. The bank has no shortfall.
Similar behaviour to us: NO → YES → NO → YES.
Just in Spanish.
That would seem Spanish to me too.

Think back to similar situations in your life. Where now, having just read the chapter and perhaps already learnt something, you can recognise that this 'plausibility thing' has kept you from or prevented you from receiving God's gift or provision.

Think about where in your life you are currently in a tight spot, where you have been stuck for a long time and write it down here - with the date!

And now simply ask Jesus for a miracle. For HIS supernatural intervention in your situation. Trust him, be curious and patient. Keep your eyes and ears open.

And write down the "arrival of the miracle" with the date. For your confirmation, encouragement, for the glory of God and that you then also have facts when you joyfully tell others about the "miracle".

Jesus is building HIS church

,,Unless the LORD builds the house,
They labour in vain who build it;"
Psalms 127 / 1a

,,Is this not the carpenter, ..."
(here we are talking about Jesus)
Mark 6 / 3a

When we founded the "Jesus Gemeinde Bamberg" in March 1991, we were rented in a commercial building; the location and the rooms were perfect for us.
Over the next few years, the church fortunately grew, also in terms of numbers.

We received more and more prophetic words and impressions from various guest preachers and also from other brothers and sisters in faith, who independently of each other and yet unanimously said that God is telling us to "enlarge our tents".

It quickly became clear what HE meant by that, because the church service room was bursting at the seams with people. We needed a larger building.

So we went on a search with Jesus, looked at various real estate, some were immediately ruled out, others seemed interesting but were cancelled at the last moment.
It was an exciting, instructive and interesting time. We continued to pray for direction on where to find the building.

One Saturday morning, I read an advert in the newspaper that piqued my interest and I immediately followed it up.
"Viewing this Saturday morning from 9am to 12pm"

Andra and I drove there straight away and had a look. A

former lamp factory, a huge site, "1000" buildings and one of them seemed perfect for us.

A hall, just after the staircase, with enough toilets and rooms for children's work, seminars and fellowship events on the upper floor.

It felt good, we walked around, looked in every corner, asked for details, numbers and got the impression that it was probably "our building".

So we met with the estate agent in the small hall and expressed our interest. We were already imagining the church service here.

He asked what purpose we had intended for it and who we were.

"Jesus Gemeinde Bamberg, a free, charismatic church, in the process of expansion to reach Bamberg and the surrounding region with the gospel of Jesus"

He liked that and suddenly said: "Have you been to the hall? That's part of it too. What do you think?"

We looked at him a little confused. "Hall? - Hello, we're standing in the middle of it"
"No, not this one. The big one"
"The big one? Which big one?"
"Well, that one, behind the double metal door"

And then I noticed the double wing door on one side wall for the first time. Even though we were in the small hall the whole time. Curious, I went over and opened one of the heavy metal doors.

I couldn't breathe. I stood rooted to the spot. I couldn't believe my eyes.
In front of me was a 700 m² hall, seven metres high, the

former high-bay warehouse. With a lorry entrance!
I was struck by an awe-inspiring atmosphere and authority, holy, almost unbearable, a heavy, divine anointing was in the room, it almost knocked me over and I knew immediately:

It was the present presence of God.

I had never felt it so intensely before. And I knew, felt, perceived - God was sitting on the other side of the hall, smiling mischievously and lovingly at me. In my spirit I heard HIM say:
"Nice that you're finally coming too. I've been waiting for you the whole time. I have this hall and the other rooms for you."

I struggled to stay on my feet, Andra felt the same way.
The decision was clear to us: we would take it. There was no other answer.

I went to the estate agent and told him of our firm interest, but we would have to ask our managing board and other church leaders before making a binding commitment.

"Yes, you have until 12 o'clock!"

We whizzed off home and thank God this property was only a few minutes away from our flat.
(That was and still is very practical for us!)

And now we had to check, to be sure. Completely sure!
We needed rock-solid clarity and certainty.

So we prayed and presented God with a "fleece", a biblical way of testing and recognising God's will.

"Fleece" originally referred to the "continuous wool of a sheep", but today it is also available in other materials.

If you want to know more about it, then look it up in the Bible, in the Old Testament, in the Book of Judges, in chapter 6, verses 36 to 40, where it describes how Gideon did it.

Gideon laid a fleece before God twice to make absolutely sure that he had understood God's will and mission exactly. He didn't want to make a mistake and drive this important matter against the wall.
And God had answered him twice in the way Gideon had presented it to HIM and asked for it. Such impossible things.

And God wasn't angry because we did this "test". He wasn't miffed because we didn't simply trust HIM. NO! HE loves it when we take HIS word and HIM seriously. HE can't say "test everything ..." and then when we test it, HE gets offended? No way!

We said to God:
" Lord, it is now Saturday morning. We know our leaders, their families and customs. They are normally all out and about now, running errands. Our experience shows that very few of them are at home or have time.
If this hall and rooms are yours, we have heard and perceived correctly, then please confirm it by arranging the following:
  – I can reach now everyone by telephone
  – everyone still has time for the viewing
  – everyone gets the same impression or words as we do, we won't tell them anything about our perception and decision in advance
  – If we don't reach ONE or ONE doesn't have a "green light" for it, then it's not from you and we'll forget the whole thing and cancel."

They were pretty impossible points, at least for us. But otherwise the seriously requested fleece makes no sense either.

"Let it be light during the day", or stuff like that. That's rubbish, it's light during the day.

As I said, it was and is a biblical principle of serious examination of a matter before God and not presumption or disrespect for God.
It was too important, too big and too important. We all had to be united and 1000 percent sure.

And the impossible happened!

- I called them all. (back then via landline ☎)
- I reached everyone immediately.
- Everyone had time and set off straight away.
- We met on site, we just told them to go in and look at everything, including the big hall, not to talk to each other, but to each ask Jesus and then we would meet again here in the car park and wanted to hear their opinions.

They swarmed out and after about 20 minutes they gradually returned to the car park.
- "This is our new church building!
- We have never experienced an anointing like the one in the great hall!
- We hear God say: This is for you!"

It was awesome.
God had responded to our fleece. HE had said the same thing to EVERYONE, to each individual, without any preliminary information from us, without any discussion between them, the Holy Spirit speaks ONE language.

Jesus had not given us a building to buy, we were open and ready for it, and actually wanted it.

But in all attempts, God closed the door, sometimes at the last minute.

But we learnt something new with every object.

We signed the rental contract with a beating and grateful heart.

Logically, we had to deal with the estate agent a few more times after that, he kept asking about the church, what the difference was to the big churches, about faith and other things.

The estate agent contact and the subsequent rental agreement became an "evangelisation event" and the end of the story was that he invited Andra and me to his home, gave his life to Jesus and we then referred him to a free church near his home. We knew this church, knew that they loved Jesus and the Holy Spirit and lived their faith.

Many years later we heard that he is still there in the church. Hallelujah! Thank you Jesus!

This is how our adventure with the "carpenter's son" began. JESUS the master builder of HIS church.

And here it's even very practical. Of course - carpentry is a trade where hands-on work is required.

With ideas, muscles, overall with a folding rule in the side pocket, spit in their hands and set off with enthusiasm and passion.

Just a carpenter!

And under HIS direction and supervision, grace and protection, strength and provision, we were able to help tackle, renovate, create - and marvel and experience miracles.

A jolt went through the whole church.

A spirit of optimism, expectation, zest for action, great joy, that is the church of Jesus, Jesus - Gemeinde!

Preparation:

We had been wondering all those months before who Jesus had brought into the church. There were craftsmen, painters, an architect, simply new brothers and sisters - we were delighted. And the donations to the church rose sharply. Remarkable!

Claro! ☺

But somehow we didn't realise why these people and the donations were actually coming. And only later did we realise that God had sent them, with their abilities, to help with the renovation of the new church building. That's how foresighted Jesus is and he really can do it.

Andra and I took over the construction management because we already had private renovation experience and my profession as a police officer of many years' standing meant that I had no fear of the "official authorisation jungle". I knew their language and their idiosyncrasies and knew how to deal with them. And we got our permission "change of use, from former industrial facilities with high-bay warehouses to church meeting rooms"
PRAISE JESUS!

So we planned, discussed, prayed, checked, discarded, re-planned, bought materials, asked questions, drew up sections, work plans and times, and, and, and, and → and then got started.
We renovated for almost a year, but moved as soon as possible, with church life and services taking place in the building site. It was an exciting, blessed and beautiful time. And quite exhausting. I think between my police shifts, we lived and worked on the church building site.

And GLORY TO JESUS - we didn't have a construction or work accident.

On one of our trips to Israel, we went on a sightseeing tour and visited a Bible museum. There it was explained to us that the function of the carpenter, because it was also about the person of Jesus, was not only the specialist of timber in the sense of cutting beams, but that at the time of Jesus, the "carpenter" was a builder, a constructor, a building contractor. The carpenter built entire houses. This was a new revelation for us and we saw Jesus in a completely new light.

HE is the master builder of our lives.

HE does not just pull in a beam, but HE builds our house of life. HE builds our faith HE is responsible for the complete measure, HE has and HE does it with passion and HE does it carefully and HE does it one hundred percent successfully.

We were also travelling with this image of Jesus as a master builder when we renovated the church and for the first time we really realised that this passage in the Bible, where Jesus says, "I will build my church..." is not only meant spiritually, but can also be understood in a very practical way.

And HE paid for everything. In advance.
Just like the well-known phrase:

Whoever orders - also pays!

And we experienced miracle after miracle in connection with the church renovation. I would like to describe a few special episodes here.

And as I said: all real, all experienced, no fake, no fiction, no science fiction, but simply the hand of our God in action for HIS CHURCH.
All honour to him for this!

Where are the 'construction sites' in your life?
Or in the church you are in?
Have you been looking for new facilities for a long time?

And you are now realising that you didn't involve the 'builder' enough, that you didn't trust him enough. You were just caught up in the logic - 'the property market isn't offering anything at the moment, it's too tight'.

Remember the maxim:
*There is always the right property available
on the "Builder Property Market",*
there is just too little asked for it!

Concrete - lorry gets stuck

During the renovation of the church hall, we needed a concrete lorry to pour the stage. We contacted the boss of the company, who came himself to see how big the lorry could be so that it would fit through the gateway. He measured it out and then wanted to send two small concrete lorries to make sure it would work.

When the day of concreting arrived, we had prepared everything, a large concrete lorry arrived contrary to expectations and agreements, and it drove through the gate without any problems, heavily loaded with several cubic metres of concrete.

We poured the concrete slab of the platform, after a while the drum of the concrete lorry was empty and the driver wanted to go back outside.

When he stood in front of the gate and wanted to drive through, he realised that he could no longer get through because the empty concrete drum had now been pushed out of the shock absorbers of the concrete mixer and the truck was now too high at the rear. There was about 20 centimetres too much vehicle height, so that the lorry could no longer get out of the hall.

We stood around at a loss and thought about how we could make the lorry lower.

Our ideas were pretty funny. We thought about letting the air out of the tyres, which would lower it, but we didn't know how to inflate the tyres again afterwards.

We considered breaking open the lintel of the gate, but then we would have caused structural damage.

And the considerations went in all possible directions, but in the end we came to no conclusion.

The lorry driver was completely frustrated and started swearing and swearing at us, which of course we told him not to do because it was a church hall and he obeyed, but was also completely baffled and grumbled angrily to himself.

In the end, it occurred to us that we could pray. Usually you don't realise it until the end or too late. You could save yourself a lot of trouble and frustration. And so we did it straight away (or finally?) and asked God to take care of the matter and somehow get the truck out.

And God answered straight away.
Suddenly, the lorry drum was pushed down as if by an invisible hand. The lorry went down about 25 centimetres and remained in this position. We stared stunned at what was happening before our eyes. There were about five or six of us from the church who witnessed it.

We realised that NOW was the time from God to act.

We all shouted for the driver, who had also got out of the lorry at a complete loss and was running around like a frightened chicken.
We shouted to the lorry driver that he should drive outside straight away.

The driver also saw this miracle, turned pale and speechless, jumped into his lorry and drove it carefully through the gate.

He stopped outside, got out again because of the paperwork (still white as a sheet, or as the Bambergers say: "keesweiß im Gsichd") and we all stared at the concrete drum again, which slowly rose out of the coach springs before our eyes until it was back to normal vehicle height, as if the invisible hand had been removed from this drum.

We wanted to explain to the driver what had just happened here, God's intervention, miracles, Jesus is alive and so on, but he fled with his lorry as if stung by a tarantula. I think he was really afraid of this God, of this church.

WOW - we knew and saw that God was with us.

Unbelievable - isn't it?
The invisible hand of God rocked the thing. Very real.

Start praying for the Holy Spirit to start fuelling your fantasy and imagination so that you can imagine the 'IMPOSSIBLE', dream about it, talk about it.

Welcome to Hebrews 11 / 1 ☺

Hello - Echo!

Another powerful story was when we experienced how God had taken care of the echo that was in the hall.

Of course, this hall was "only" a bare concrete hall, 35 metres long and 7 metres high. When we stepped into the hall for the first time, we realised that there was a huge echo in the hall.

You can imagine that if you stood at the entrance door and said "hello" and then walked slowly to the other side of the hall, i.e. 35 metres, you could still hear your own "hello". That was of course a huge problem for a service hall, because you had to capture the echo in some way to get an acceptable sound.

How would that sound in a sermon where you just start with "Hello good morning" and then you hear "Hello good morning" for a quarter of an hour, caused only by the echo.

Welcoming is all well and good and is expected, but not like this.
At the final blessing it would of course be a welcome effect if you say: "God bless you" and then you hear: "God bless you - God bless you - God bless you - you - you - you - you - you ..."
That would of course be a gag, an interesting goodbye to the service. But this wasn't about a gag.

But now we were struggling with this problem and we had to come up with a solution. Of course, our experience with the lorry had already taught us that we could (had to) pray and hope for God's supernatural help.

So we called an acoustic engineer who offered solutions specifically for meeting rooms and he came along, brought his measuring instruments to measure the various time and echo sequences and then suggested suitable solutions. He then told us roughly how much it would cost.

As I said, the man came, took his measuring instruments, shook his head and said "This really is a huge echo. I've rarely had that. To get it under control with various soundproofing measures, you would have to reckon with about 50,000 DM to turn this hall into a meeting hall with good sound and acoustics."
We thanked him for his expert advice and told him we would be in touch again.

Back then, we still had the good old, stable DEUTSCHE MARK (DM). Oh, those were the days. The changeover to the EURO only came on 1 January 2002 and many prices doubled almost overnight, but not incomes.

We started praying again and asked God for a different solution. A solution that comes from HIM and bears HIS signature. And that doesn't cost 50,000 DM.

And God gave Andra and me impressions of what we should do in terms of sound insulation.

God's humour is very special in a way!

I kept getting a picture and a word into my spirit and mind and that was:

"Pigsty".

I thought to myself: "God, this can't be from YOU, because this isn't a pigsty, it's supposed to be YOUR hall!" And yet this word and this image "pigsty" kept coming back and I realised that God was trying to tell me something. So I asked Jesus what it was all about.

And HE said to me: "Günther, remember when you were a teenager, you used to help out with a brother from your church, he was a farmer, he had a big pigsty and how was this pigsty soundproofed?"

Suddenly it came back to me. After 29 years. I had never thought about it again. But luckily I have Jesus - HE doesn't forget anything.

Except for the sins that I have confessed to HIM and HE has forgiven me. They are forgotten with HIM! Thanks to God.

„If we confess our sins,
He is faithful and just to forgive us our sins
and to cleanse us from all unrighteousness. "
1 John 1 / 9

„having wiped out the handwriting of requirements
that was against us, which was contrary to us.
And He has taken it out of the way,
having nailed it to the cross. "
Colossians 2 / 14

„For I will be merciful to their unrighteousness,
and their sins and their lawless deeds
I will remember no more." "
Hebrews 8 / 12

Erased, forgiven and forgotten, what a blessing.
This is so important to know that my sin is washed away and forgiven and forgotten by the blood of Jesus.

We are constantly plagued with condemnation by One, the devil, who wants to persuade us that we are guilty forever.
No way!
Forgiveness through Jesus is guaranteed if I and you come to Jesus and ask for it and confess it to HIM.

WOW! Free! No more damnation!
Devil - shut up!

> *"There is therefore now no condemnation to those*
> *who are in Christ Jesus,*
> *who do not walk according to the flesh,*
> *but according to the Spirit. "*
> Romans 8 / 1

But let's get back to the "pigsty".
I had asked the farmer about this material that was on the walls and ceilings, which I hadn't known about myself.

The farmer explained to me that it was "Heraklith". These were lightweight slabs of pressed wood wool. Slabs 2 metres long, 50 centimetres wide, bound with cement so that they were also fireproof. This surface was so rough that it absorbed the sound enormously and suddenly I realised what God wanted to tell me with "pigsty".

HE had reminded me of this time on the farm so that I could make the connection and I remembered "Heraklith".

Why HE didn't just say "Heraklith" is beyond me. HE is the boss. But I had checked.

Please remember and remind me that one day in eternity we will ask God about it.

Now it was clear that we should use these Heraklith panels to bind and stop the sound on the large walls where the sound mainly bounces.

He also gave us the picture that we should cover the walls with fabric, with air cushions underneath, which would also absorb the sound and provide additional insulation.

We should also lay a carpet, a felt floor (700 square metres you know what that means), which would also contribute to sound insulation.
If the chairs were still inside, we would have optimal hall acoustics.

These were the ideas and plans of our carpenter Jesus.

Well, we weren't experts, so we didn't really know from experience whether it would work. But we trusted our builder.

> "If the Lord does not build the house,
> they labour in vain that build it!"
> (Remember this verse!)

We presented these "crazy simple plans" to our building team and church leadership and they looked at us a little askance and initially doubted their success. They told us that it would never work. If the expert was talking about special materials, then we couldn't come up with pigsty equipment.

Logic versus faith / confidence!
Once again, intelligence, logic and life experience battled against divine, illogical, unimaginable solutions.

Also with us in the church, with us charismatic Jesus freaks.
Ooh – shame on us!
But it has been and continues to be so. The process of renewing according to the passage from Romans 12 continues and must continue.

So I said to our people:
"Pay attention! We are one hundred per cent sure of what we have heard from Jesus. If it doesn't work, then we will pay the cost of what we have spent on it out of our own pockets, so that the church would not be harmed. Then we would only

have invested the working time for nothing and would be one or more experiences richer."

In the end, our faith and trust won out. They also agreed with this proposal and so we got to work, spat into our hands, sweat towel at the ready – let´s start.

Install Heraklith panels on certain walls, wall coverings, needle felt.
It was an exhausting time, always on the scaffolding or on the ground on our knees, but it went smoothly. The carpenter was with us.

Jesus opened doors with the authorities, the building authorities, the fire brigade (escape routes and emergency exits) and the landlord, gave us favour and understanding, everything went really well.
Everything is always supported by prayer and certainty:

Jesus has given us this building,
so that we can continue to build the
Jesus – Gemeinde Bamberg,
under HIS leadership
and for a great harvest
of thousands of people who will be saved,
and we are prepared.

Do you remember? "I want to build my church..."

All materials had to comply with fire protection class B1 in accordance with the official requirements and they had been prepared accordingly by the suppliers.

We always had this vision and our mission in mind and were eager to see the result. We didn't really know, we went step by step in faith, but we believed our carpenter.

DONE!

We called the specialist again, who had already helped us once. When he came into the hall, he stopped in shock and exclaimed: "For heaven's sake, what have you done! That stuff doesn't help at all!"

Our heart slipped into our trousers, our faith was shaken.
"Please measure it anyway" we asked him.

Faith and hope against a certified acoustics specialist.
Formal logic versus divine crazy solutions.

He took out his measuring device again, this time it seemed quite threatening.

Mr Specialist stared at his display, switched off, switched on again, continued to stare.
Switched off, went outside, got another measuring device, measure, stare, off, on, stare.

Bewilderment appeared on his now pale face.

"That's not possible! That can't be true! Not with that stuff on the walls!"
We asked him what was going on.

"I've measured everything several times now, two different devices. I thought one device was broken. The pointer is exactly in the centre at zero.
Zero is the best you can manage. A little more and there is echo again, less and the acoustics are dead.
Who gave you the idea for the materials?
The mixing ratio of the different surfaces?"

"The carpenter!"

"The carpenter ????"
"Yes, Jesus, the carpenter."
And then we gave him a testimony of how Jesus had given us the ideas and that HE had given us very explicit instructions.
"Unbelievable! I've never heard anything like this before. But it worked."

And as a conclusion to this miraculous experience: the cost of our heavenly acoustic measure was a fraction of what the specialist had estimated for his measures.

Jesus - YOU are the best.
You are the Champion of Carpenters!!!!

Disco meets Church:

„Praise the LORD!
Praise God in His sanctuary;
Praise Him in His mighty firmament!
Praise Him for His mighty acts;
Praise Him according to His excellent greatness!
Praise Him with the sound of the trumpet;
Praise Him with the lute and harp!
Praise Him with the timbrel and dance;
Praise Him with stringed instruments and flutes!
Praise Him with loud cymbals;
Praise Him with clashing cymbals!
Let everything that has breath praise the LORD.
Praise the LORD!
Psalms 150

„Oh, sing to the LORD a new song!
For He has done marvelous things;
His right hand and His holy arm
have gained Him the victory.
The LORD has made known His salvation;
His righteousness He has revealed
in the sight of the nations.
He has remembered His mercy and His faithfulness
to the house of Israel;
All the ends of the earth have seen the salvation of our God.
Shout joyfully to the LORD, all the earth;
Break forth in song, rejoice, and sing praises.
Sing to the LORD with the harp,
With the harp and the sound of a psalm,
With trumpets and the sound of a horn;
Shout joyfully before the LORD, the King.“
Psalms 98 / 1 – 6

The English King James translation puts it a little more slangly, not quite so "pious":

> *„ Make a **joyful noise** unto the LORD,*
> *all the earth: Make a **loud noise**,*
> *and rejoice, and sing praise.*
> *Sing unto the LORD with the harp;*
> *With the harp, and the voice of a psalm.*
> *With trumpets and sound of cornet.*
> *Make a **joyful noise** before the LORD, the King."*

In other words, the call to make a "joyful noise" to the Lord, our King. A loud noise! We are asked to do this THREE times in these few verses.

With timpani and trumpets, so to speak, everything we have, all in! To the honour of our Father in heaven.

He didn't have to tell us twice!
HE seems to like it.
No funeral music, no memorial services.
Not in the HOUSE OF GOD!
NO → JOYFUL CELEBRATIONS!

Rejoicing in our God. Enthusiasm about Jesus, drunk in the Holy Spirit, so that we can no longer stand. Laughing, shouting - full power.

God obviously loves that.
It was the same at Pentecost. It was practically the first church service. You can read the action story in the Acts of the Apostles, chapter 2. The Holy Spirit makes the noise and all the outside.

120 people gathered, prayed to the Lord, the Holy Spirit rushed in with such a roar that almost the whole town ran together. He fills the first church to such an extent that some

of the spectators thought: "They are all drunk!".

I wonder what they thought?
Staggering, laughing merrily, falling over, speaking incomprehensible words, lying in each other's arms, cheering, singing, hanging quietly and laying in the corner?

That could just as easily be an observation from the last shooting or fire brigade festival. I have often experienced this in this form when we were on duty at public festivals.

But I have seen exactly the same thing in church services all over the world after the Holy Spirit has come upon people with power. It is called the "power of the Spirit".

Peter briefly explains what's going on here, Jesus and the gospel, and calls for a decision. Wow. Without a choir and an emotional song, without "we'll all close our eyes now".

"Hey guys! I have explained to you here what is going on, without Jesus you are lost forever. And all the outside stuff here, including the "drunkenness" symptoms, comes from the Holy Spirit as confirmation.
Even the old prophets we know so well described what you see here. So it is normal from now on because the Holy Spirit has been poured out today.
Who wants to take Jesus into their life and be saved? Show of hands please!"

WUMM! 2000 hands rush up to the sky. WOW! What a result for a Holy Spirit-orchestrated noise evangelisation. Without flyers, social media - nada. Just a Holy Spirit meeting!
I wonder if we can learn anything?

And shortly afterwards, 120 disciples baptised the 2,000 new converts in water. Following the example of Jesus. By complete immersion with their own free will and decision. Without waiting or checking whether they were serious. Simply baptised. All 2000 of them into the water. And into the church. The 120 had their hands full. Hallelujah!

And that's why a proper church needs a proper sound. Proclamation of the word and musical praise. Full speed ahead with the instruments and microphones. Thanks to the biblical model. Decibels are a "must have".
What do you think will happen in heaven one day when we stand directly in front of Jesus and an immense crowd of people plus the angels look at HIM enthusiastically, gratefully, happily and adoringly?
The cheer rolls! And it won't be quiet, I promise you!

How many decibels do you think the praise will have when millions and millions of redeemed people worship, cheer and celebrate their Redeemer and Saviour?
You'd better take earplugs with you.

Now we had created the conditions.
Pointer to zero - do you remember?
Sure, your short-term memory is ok.

I mean, 4900 cubic metres of space need to be filled with sound. Illuminated. So that it looks and sounds good.
We could no longer score points with our old system. Something else was needed.

According to expert offers, we again had to reckon with about 50,000 DM for sound and light.

And off again to the "carpenter".
HE, who had preached in front of thousands of people without a microphone, didn't need it.
Because the universe trembles, obeys and bows before HIS voice.

„ Give unto the LORD, O you mighty ones,
Give unto the LORD glory and strength.
Give unto the LORD the glory due to His name;
Worship the LORD in the beauty of holiness.
The voice of the LORD is over the waters;
The God of glory thunders;
The LORD is over many waters.
The voice of the LORD is powerful;
The voice of the LORD is full of majesty.
The voice of the LORD breaks the cedars,
Yes, the LORD splinters the cedars of Lebanon.
He makes them also skip like a calf,
Lebanon and Sirion like a young wild ox.
The voice of the LORD divides the flames of fire.
The voice of the LORD shakes the wilderness;
The LORD shakes the Wilderness of Kadesh.“
Psalms 29 / 1 - 8
(Sirion is a country name for Mount Hermon,
on the Syrian - Lebanese - Israeli border)

There is power in the voice of the Lord.
Jesus doesn't need a light show because he is the light of the
world, the shining morning star!

„ I, Jesus, have sent My angel
to testify to you these things in the churches.
I am the Root and the Offspring of David,
the Bright and Morning Star.“ “
Revelation 22 / 16

„ Then Jesus spoke to them again, saying,
I am the light of the world.
He who follows Me shall not walk in darkness,
but have the light of life.”
John 8 / 12

Hold on tight! Better fasten your seatbelt! Put on your sunglasses, or even better, your welding goggles.
It's better to have Jesus as your friend and saviour!

JESUS is the inventor and creator of acoustics and light.
(among other things)
The chief expert, so to speak. The carpenter who knows EVERYTHING because HE invented and created it.
(not Ricola* from Switzerland!)

JESUS!

„He is the image of the invisible God,
the firstborn over all creation.
For by Him all things were created
that are in heaven and that are on earth,
visible and invisible,
whether thrones or dominions or principalities or powers.
All things were created through Him and for Him.
And He is before all things,
and in Him all things consist.
And He is the head of the body, the church,
who is the beginning, the firstborn from the dead,
that in all things He may have the preeminence.
Colossians 1 / 15 – 18

The everlasting number

1

JESUS!

We prayed again and asked for HIS "WONDER - FULL" solution.
We were pretty relaxed and yet excited, curious to see what HE would show us this time.

A few days later, a brother from the church, who was also fully involved in the construction team, came to us and said: "An old friend called me. Until a few years ago, he had a large discotheque in the Bamberg district, but had given it up. He had stored all of his sound and lighting equipment and now wanted to sell it. Would that be something for us? That looks like the answer."

"Have a look at all the stuff and ask him if everything works and what he wants for it."

We sent the brother off with this order, he knew his way around things pretty well, he had a show band before he came to Jesus, with which he travelled all over Germany.

"Everything ok, a bit dusty because it was stored in a barn, functional as far as I could check. Fully equipped with lights, sound, effects and so on."

"Yes, and the price?" It sounded great.

"5,000 is what he wants."

We prayed, presented it to "our carpenter" and Jesus gave us the green light. It was his arrangement for us.

And so we collected everything, cleaned it of dust and chicken feathers (they were also running around in the barn), tested everything before we assembled it, laid kilometres of cables, and so on and so forth.

And then the first full test. Full steam ahead. Turned up and switched on. Light's on!

Mamma Mia!

Hey man! I tell you, you really thought you were at the disco. (ok, it wasn't difficult to think that way - was it?)
A super sound. A light show at its best.

The bass speakers under the stage stairs almost pushed the first row of chairs away. They had the power to lift your toupee and make your stubbly hair flutter in the wind.

I think we were the only church in Germany at the time with a disco ball, fog machines, strobe lights, black lights and other light machines.
And all for 5000 DM.

And they worked perfectly, some of them are still in use today, 20 years later.
We can rejoice, dance and jump for joy and excitement about our Saviour, Deliverer, Healer, Carpenter - Hallelujah Jesus.

Over the next few years, we wrote several children's musicals and the entire sound and lighting equipment was a huge blessing when performing in church. Bam!

It's clear that we don't go full blast all the time. We normally drive at an acceptable and pleasant volume. Logo*.
We don't want to annoy or drive away our visitors to the services, who come from all age groups. And not constantly praying against ear problems that we might have caused ourselves.
But we could if we wanted!
And we would be allowed to if we wanted to.

Think of the joyful noise, the loud noise. ☺

So you are welcome to come, even without earplugs or fear that we will "blow you out" of the door again.

God can be loud or quiet,
gentle or powerful.
We can't exclude any of them.

Torrential rain obeys the name of Jesus

When we talk about the miracles that Jesus performed, there is a well-known example from the Bible where He commands the storm to be calm. **And the storm had to obey his word.** Read it yourself.

> *„On the same day, when evening had come,*
> *He (Jesus) said to them,*
> *Let us cross over to the other side.*
> *Now when they had left the multitude,*
> *they took Him along in the boat as He was.*
> *And other little boats were also with Him.*
> *And a great windstorm arose,*
> *and the waves beat into the boat,*
> *so that it was already filling.*
> *But He was in the stern, asleep on a pillow.*
> *And they awoke Him and said to Him,*
> *Teacher, do You not care that we are perishing?*
> *Then He arose and rebuked the wind,*
> *and said to the sea,*
> *Peace, be still!*
> *And the wind ceased and there was a great calm.*
> *But He said to them,*
> *Why are you so fearful?*
> *How is it that you have no faith?*
> *And they feared exceedingly, and said to one another,*
> *Who can this be, that even the wind and the sea obey Him!"*
> Mark 4 / 35 – 41

That must have been really impressive. Just in the middle of a storm, mortal danger, the howling of the storm, soaking wet to the bone, bailing water like a world champion, screaming, panic, helplessness in the face of the forces of nature. Panic sends its regards.

And you think you're safe because you have Jesus on board. (Man - man - man!)
And what does Jesus do? HE is asleep! Excuse me - HE is asleep?
With the storm? With the noise? With the water thundering into the boat?

YES!!!
Jesus knew that all this could not kill him.
HE is the prince of life. HE is life itself. Life in person. As its creator, HE stands above the forces of nature.

> *,,Therefore My Father loves Me,*
> *because I lay down My life that I may take it again.*
> ***No one takes it from Me,***
> *but I lay it down of Myself.*
> *I have power to lay it down,*
> *and I have power to take it again.*
> *This command I have received from My Father. "*
> John 10 / 17 + 18

No storm and no waves could harm Jesus, they tried, but – NO WAY!

> *,,For the wages of sin is death,*
> *but the gift of God is eternal life*
> *in Christ Jesus our Lord. "*
> Romans 6 / 23

> *,,For we do not have a High Priest*
> *who cannot sympathize with our weaknesses,*
> *but was in all points tempted as we are,*
> ***yet without sin. "***
> *Hebrews 4 / 15*

Sin $\rightarrow$ death! Inevitable. You will receive this wage automatically.

No sin → no death! Logo*! ☺

That's a very important sentence - we'll come to it later.

So nothing and no one could take Jesus' life. No stoning attempt, no murder plot, no storm! Not even later on the cross. HE gave it up voluntarily, himself, out of love for you and me, sacrificed it.

And that's why HE could sleep peacefully.

But the followers of Jesus, those who were there, were really shaken up, both naturally and in their faith. What's the point now?

"We are all in the same boat"

YES, but it depends on what you do. Give up, resign, go down with the masses or remember Jesus and HIS words and at least try to imitate HIM. That is often the problem. We look at the others. What are they doing? If they are in the same situation and react in the same way, we think it's normal because everyone does it that way. The majority is RIGHT! Think again!

The disciples' boat was not the only one in the storm. Other boats with people who knew Jesus and were following him (of course, otherwise they wouldn't have travelled in their boats) were nearby and also in the storm. Logical, right? (Here the logic may have a say. Ok!)

Everyone is fighting, everyone is panicking, everyone is looking over to the boat where Jesus is simply sleeping. Like under a cheese bell. No noise, no getting wet, rocked violently to sleep.

And they wait to be rescued. But nothing happens - for the moment.

Isn't it a stupid thing to believe?

Another well-known story of Jesus is similar.
(Matthew 14 / 24 - 29)
The disciples in the boat, Jesus will follow later, HE says.
(HELLO - ?, the ferry connections had just been cancelled
because of the storm), exactly - storm, waves, boat full,
trousers and nappy full, fear, panic, screaming. Just the
normal madness. Again. Goodbye - good life.

And then Jesus comes! Running across the water as if it were
the promenade. Without lights and reflector waistcoat
(because it was pitch dark). But the road traffic regulations
for the behaviour of pedestrians (§ 25 StVO = german law*)
only apply to the road, not to the water. It doesn't apply here.
And pedestrians on the water are not provided for in the
water navigation regulations.
So next time you're walking on the water at night, feel free to
leave your lantern at home! ☺

And suddenly the dripping wet Peter in the boat realises that
the thing with Jesus is somehow different. And that faith
moves mountains. That should also work with the crests of
waves or something.

Boldness of faith flows through his veins, courage and
determination. Spiritual adrenaline and natural too.
Blood pressure rises to the max. almost into the red zone,
ALMOST!
But let's hear it in the original - tone of the Bible.

*„But the boat was now in the middle of the sea, tossed by the
waves, for the wind was contrary.
Now in the fourth watch of the night Jesus went to them,
walking on the sea. And when the disciples saw Him walking
on the sea, they were troubled, saying, "It is a ghost!" And
they cried out for fear.
But immediately Jesus spoke to them, saying,*

"Be of good cheer! It is I; do not be afraid."
And Peter answered Him and said, "Lord, if it is You,
command me to come to You on the water."
So He said, "Come." And when Peter had come down out of
the boat, he walked on the water to go to Jesus.
Matthew 14 / 24 – 29

"All in the same boat" - and ONE person does it differently. He takes the initiative of faith, he puts the word of Jesus into practice, courageously, he gets out of the lurching boat (that was already a masterstroke), practically walking not on water, but on the word of Jesus. And the word carries. Despite waves, despite storms, despite physical laws or not.
At least as long as he is focussed on Jesus and his word.

I think the other companions in the boat were really knocked out. Their lower jaws dropped to their knees.
"That's not possible! That can't be true! No such thing!"

That's awesome! Peter - just like a droned rat and now he boldly climbs out of the boat and runs towards Jesus. What a chap! What an experience and adventure.

In the end, he let his focus be distracted. Logic really blew up in his face. Suddenly he no longer sees Jesus and his word that carries him, but the wind and the waves.

"Water has no beams, that's what grandad always told me."
(= instilled, seriously suggested, conveyed)
Suddenly he feels the wet hair on his face, the howling of the wind in his ears, the storm tearing at his wet clothes. Now he realises it - not before?

„But when he saw that the wind was strong, he was afraid;
and beginning to sink he cried out, saying,
"Lord, save me!" ...

*... And immediately Jesus stretched out His hand and caught
him, and said to him,*
"O you of little faith, why did you doubt?"
*And when they got into the boat, the wind ceased.
Then those who were in the boat came and worshiped Him,
saying, "Truly You are the Son of God."*
Matthew 14 / 30 – 33

The wrong focus, the "natural" perception, this "it can't be"
has literally pulled this plank of Jesus' word out from under
his feet and then he is back in his learnt, logical, normal, all
the world does it this way - ground, er - water.
And then water has no beams. We all know that. It's always
been like that. So there you go. Logic has won.
Goodbye - chuckle chuckle.

And Jesus saves him. Pulls him out, puts him back on his feet
and on the water again. Why doesn't Jesus sink? Surely the
wind and the waves annoy HIM too?

Peter! What, again? You've just been embarrassingly sunk
and now you have to try again?
Yes, but this time at the hand of Jesus. Perhaps you noticed
while reading that it doesn't say that Jesus let go of Peter's
hand. Fortunately. Both are now standing on faith. The faith
of Jesus. That holds. Is stronger than water and the laws of
nature.
Faith in Jesus holds - 1000 percent!

So we see that the Word of God as a gangplank changes the
focus. Takes the power out of circumstances, changes fear
into boldness and trust. Makes the impossible possible. Lets
us go from the "natural" to the "supernatural". But only
through HIS word. It is also called "faith".

In both reports, Jesus is disappointed in his disciples.

"You of little faith"

HE says. You can literally hear the disappointment in his voice.

"You of little faith"

Well, that's not really praise or comfort.

"Hey Jesus - that's not really nice of you! You have to look at the whole situation, the seriousness of the hour and all that. The storm is particularly severe today. They already said so in the weather forecast and so did the storm warning service! The app said: "Don't go out on the water!" And did you see the waves? Giant - O man! So to talk about "little faith" now is a bit harsh and unfair - isn't it?"

Strangely enough, Jesus does not accept this.

And stay calm! HE does not say: "You unbelievers". Then they or we would not believe in HIM at all.

"You of little faith"

that means: little trust in HIM, in HIS word. Seeing the world's standard, its logic, as the highest level and acting accordingly. And disregarding the level of faith in action, the supernatural possibilities as believers in Jesus. Jesus had "EXPECTED" it from them.
They could have taken it into their own hands, in the name of Jesus. In faith. They could also have helped their mates and fellow believers and sufferers. They would also have benefited and learnt. But they couldn't get out of their "logic boat".
And that is often our problem.

How often has Jesus unfortunately had to say to me: "Günther - You of little faith"

So what is the word of God and Jesus' commission to us? To me? What does HE expect of me - in faith?

> *„ Most assuredly, I say to you,*
> *he who believes in Me,*
> *the works that I do he will do also;*
> *and greater works than these he will do,*
> *because I go to My Father. "*
> John 14 / 12

What Jesus says here and what he means is really quite blatant. And also expects us to do it!

Well, Jesus is just a little different, simply supernatural. So naturally supernatural.

Well - you will think to yourself now. Am I Jesus?

Thank God not. There can only be ONE. Inimitable, unique, eternal, powerful, loving, miracle-working, redeeming, forgiving, ...

But wait! What is Jesus actually saying here?

We will do it, ...

… if we believe in HIM.

Not:
- − perhaps
- − sometimes
- − a few special ones
- − when we have gathered enough courage
- − are old enough in faith
- − have acquired certificates of faith

No! **"He who believes in me..."** says Jesus. HE simply assumes that. Really blatant.

Jesus has not the slightest doubt that if we "truly believe in HIM", we will do it 100%.

Which, conversely, would mean that if we don't do it, we "don't really believe in Jesus" and trust HIM?
Or is that too harsh or wrongly formulated?

We should think about this because Jesus himself often uses this formulation. Think again about the Great Commission from Mark 16.
That is exciting and challenging.

And Jesus also says here: JUST BELIEVE!

No theological studies are necessary at all.

JUST BELIEVE!

No special calling or gift.

JUST BELIEVE!

No need to be a believer for 30 years or more.

JUST BELIEVE!

Not seeing my knowledge, experience and what I have learnt as the highest level and irrevocable limit.

JUST BELIEVE! ...

… Trust HIM and HIS Word and Holy Spirit
… and **DOING**.

Here again for clarification: The points just mentioned are all correct, good and helpful. It is great if you walk with Jesus throughout your life, if God gives you special gifts and callings, if you study the Word of God - day and night.
But they are absolutely not preconditions for what Jesus says.
So don't hide behind it, don't look for excuses, no matter how pious they sound. Sorry!!

Give it some thought, read the Bible and write down what Jesus has done.

That's going to be a pretty long list.
YOUR list! YOUR "to do - list"!

"...will also do the works that I do..."
This is the challenge, the thrill, the test for you (if you want it and accept it) and for me. Again and again.
Mamma Mia!

Let me help you start this list. What do we read in the New Testament - what has Jesus done - the "works"? Don't make it too complicated.
For example:

- HE prayed, sometimes whole nights → that is a "WORK"
- proclaimed the kingdom of God
- had fellowship with the disciples
- laid hands on the sick for healing
- ... → from here you can continue yourself
  You don't have to continue directly with the feeding of the 5000 or walking on water, but please don't forget! Put these points more to the end of the list. ☺

And then start praying and asking the Holy Spirit to help you do it. To remind you, to give you ideas to do it, opportunities, boldness and faith in results because you have done what Jesus did - in simple faith.

And as a small comfort and encouragement:
The disciples of Jesus in the Bible did not study theology either.
Learning by seeing, hearing and doing – doing by faith!
That was the motto. That was all.
Learning by doing, imitating, in faith. Brilliant.
Jesus did not found a theological university. HE founded faith in your heart.

HE did not give you thousands of theological books so that you would learn them by heart. HE has "only" given you the Bible - HIS word.

Wow - that's a load off my mind, or two or three.

One day, Jesus surprised us with a provocation. Today we say "challenge", which sounds more modern and cooler. But it's the same thing. Doing something unusual that you've never done before.

We have an older house, three-storey, built around 1890 and there are always a few things to do.

Years ago, the roof had to be redone and to cut a long story short, Andra and I did it ourselves. We saved about DM 20,000 (approx. € 10,000) and that was a great profit for 4 weeks' work.

So we got the materials, set up the scaffolding, found out what we had to watch out for, checked the weather forecast and waited for the right day to uncover the roof.

The right day has come! Weather forecast reports cloudless skies for the next few days, zero percent chance of rain. ☺
This is our time. Thank you Jesus - that's what we prayed for. A great answer to prayer.

Thank the Lord for reliable weather reports. Logical.

We started very early, uncovered a large part of the roof and took down the old battens. We wanted to re-batten and re-cover this part. A day's work.

When this part was uncovered and we were about to start battening, the "challenge" began.

Suddenly a strong wind came up, black clouds appeared on

the horizon and became ever blacker and more threatening, racing towards us. It seemed as if they were mocking us. They attacked us. Attack!!!
We stood in our open roof, between the roof beams and could hardly believe it.

"But the weather forecast had said otherwise. We had prayed for good weather. And we had already given thanks for the forecast good weather!"

The black wall of clouds came closer and you could already see the heavy rain coming down. The whole sky was suddenly black. Not a bit of blue left, no sun to be seen.

And we are on our open roof.

Andra and I looked at each other.
"When this downpour hits us, the water runs in upstairs and out the door on the ground floor."

Remember: old house! Wooden ceilings, three floors, each floor inhabited and furnished. What a disaster.

Getting a huge tarpaulin up and stretching it - too late!
We could already hear the sound of the rain. And it was getting closer and closer. Everything was black. The catastrophe was already greeting us and laughing at us. Taunting and mocking us.
Well, that's it! ☹

"Jesus - HELP", we cried out to the Lord Jesus.

Neighbours' heads appeared behind the neighbouring windows, they knew of our plan, knew that we were now on the open roof and were now witnessing our "deluge".

"You have the authority of my name!
Use it!
Command the rain to depart. Threaten him!
Stand firm. Do not leave the roof!"

Completely surprised, we both heard Jesus speaking in our minds and hearts. And we immediately remembered Jesus in the boat and Peter on the water.

„And they (the disciples) came to Him (Jesus)
and awoke Him, saying,
"Master, Master, we are perishing!"
(This can also happen on the roof)
Then He (Jesus) *arose and rebuked the wind*
and the raging of the water.
And they ceased, and there was a calm."
Luke 8 / 24

„ So He (Jesus) *said, "Come."*
And when Peter had come down out of the boat,
he walked on the water to go to Jesus.
But when he saw that the wind was strong,
he was afraid; and beginning to sink he cried out, saying,
"Lord, save me!"
And immediately Jesus stretched out His hand
and caught him, and said to him,
"O you of little faith, why did you doubt?"
And when they got into the boat, the wind ceased.
Then those who were in the boat came and worshiped Him,
saying :Truly You are the Son of God."
Matthew 14 / 29 – 32
(remember, we already had this scripture!)

The black wall came closer, laughing at us two little figures. It poured from buckets, oh what am I saying - from bathtubs!

We saw the torrents rushing along the gutter of the street. You could have surfed on them.

20 metres - the wall of rain came towards us. Like a curtain. Like a malicious monster that wanted to wash us off the roof.

"In Jesus' name,
Rain - you will not touch our house.
We forbid it in the name of Jesus!"

We stretched out our hand against the black wall and threatened it! Yes - we threatened it. Boldness, faith and certainty flowed through us.

"Heads up, attention!
LOGIC to Kunsti's over here:
("Kunsti" is the short form of our last name)
This is ridiculous!
I'll remind you who's in charge here.
I'm the boss!"

"Heads up, attention!
Here Kunsti's to LOGIC:
In Jesus' name, it will not touch our house.
We threaten the black wall in faith,
according to the word of God
and with the power of the name of Jesus!
Jesus is the Boss – not you!"

"LOGIC to Kunsti's over here:
This is useless,
look at the masses of water
and see the storm wind"
(the trees bent, leaves flew and the water was running)

"Here Kunsti's to LOGIC:
We don't look at it, even though we see it.
We look at Jesus and his word!
We do not give way, in Jesus' name!
black wall - YOU have to give way,
YOU must obey the name of Jesus!"

10 metres - The black waterfall came towards us.
Faith in the reliability of the word of Jesus, the power of HIS wonderful name, joy and certainty of victory pumped even more strongly through our veins and filled our hearts.

The horrified faces of the neighbours were still behind the windows.

„Then Moses stretched out his hand over the sea;
and the LORD caused the sea to go back
by a strong east wind all that night,
and made the sea into dry land,
and the waters were divided.
So the children of Israel went
into the midst of the sea on the dry ground,
and the waters were a wall to them
on their right hand and on their left. "
Exodus 14 / 21 + 22

And suddenly the black wall of clouds tore open just in front of our house.

I'm telling you, it was like a film. Unbelievable, but true. Steven Spielberg or James Cameron couldn't have made it more dramatic and exciting.

This deep black, closed rain cloud opened up at the last second, parted and passed to the right and left of our house.

Above us, suddenly blue sky again. The border between BLACK and BLUE, as if drawn with a ruler. As if with a knife, cut out of the black, threatening and destructive mass of clouds. Precise, surgically perfect.

We were at the highest point on the roof. We could see everything around us. 360 degree panoramic view.
"Circarama - cinema at its best.

Everything black all round, end of the world, deluge! Above us, a window to the sky. A patch of blue. A blue oasis. As if Jesus wanted to see better.

We were still standing there with our hands outstretched, we looked at each other, stunned at first, then we grinned, then we cheered for our Jesus. A cry of victory echoed over the rooftops of our neighbourhood, over Bamberg.

The black cloud was angry, offended, it dropped water like crazy. You could also say it wet its pants out of fear of the proclaimed name of Jesus and two small, but threatening, outstretched hands on the roof. And how! In torrents!

But not on our house. Not even on our terrace, our garden. Our property.
At the neighbours, everything wet. Total rain.

We have blue sky and everything is dry.
Ha - Ha! Devil. There's nothing! Awww - awww!

And behind our property, shortly after the garden fence, this "open cloud eye" closed again. The cloud was closed again, jet black and continued on its humiliated way, continuing to wet its pants.

It immediately reminded us of how Moses had parted the Red Sea so that God's people could pass through on dry land. And there was water to the right and left. We just had the Bible passage.

The people of Israel were hunted by Pharaoh, he wanted to enslave them again. He had driven them to the edge of the Red Sea.
Military, strategic, logical - perfectly done.
No way out, surrender or drown!
"Highway to Hell!

But he had not reckoned with God and HIS Moses.

"Stretch out your hand over the sea"

God told Moses.
On other occasions, Moses should stretch out his ROD. Here the hand.

In the Bible, the rod symbolises authority. A simple version of a sceptre. But no less effective.
Or the hand.

Said and done.
And the sea parted. A huge corridor was created between the two banks.

Space for almost 1 million people. This is what Bible experts assume. The people of Israel had been in slavery for 400 years and had multiplied so much that Pharaoh was afraid they might overrun the Egyptians.

And now they travelled with men and women, old and young, carts and carriages, mothers with children by the hand, grandmas and grandpas with their walking sticks, supported by their grandchildren, sheep, chickens and goats, simply dry-shod, through this God-created sea corridor.
For them it became a "Highway to Salvation"!

From the shore of death, hopelessness and re-enslavement to the shore of salvation, hope and the promised land.
Made by God.
What a powerful image of salvation through Jesus, water baptism and our eternal destination.

I can imagine the fish of the Red Sea, the water is crystal clear and there are fish in abundance and in all colours and sizes, they hung with their noses on these two water walls to the right and left of the corridor and were amazed.

"Mother - get the children. They have to see this. The relatives will never believe us when they come to visit on Sunday. Take a selfie! That's never happened before!
What's going on there?"

With God, yes! ☺ HE is the God of miracles. The MAKER of the IMPOSSIBLE!
Hallelujah - All glory to the name of Jesus.
You can read the whole story in Exodus chapter 14. Pure action - with a happy ending!

So a happy ending only for the people of Israel and Moses, Pharaoh and his henchmen had thought that as an unbelieving ruler serving a thousand gods he could simply sit on Moses' experience of faith and carry out his demonic, deadly plan.
Far from it!

He drove with horse and chariots, general staff and army, simply on the "Highway to Salvation", it's that simple. Never mind. God is dead. You can go ahead and insult HIM. Ignore HIM and all HIS old-fashioned stuff, mock HIM.

And Moses, at God's command, stretched his hand across the sea again and the waters flowed back together, goodbye corridor, goodbye Pharaoh, with man and mouse, er horse, dead. Mouse dead. Or is it now called horse death? I don't know exactly. In any case, for him, the great Pharaoh, it became the "Highway to Hell".

If archaeological reports are to be believed, artefacts of Egyptian weapons and chariots have been found in the sea at a narrow part of the Red Sea where it is not so deep. What are Egyptian chariots and weapons doing in the middle of the sea? That would mean that the biblical account is real. Pretty cool, right?

The perfidious plan had not worked. Pharaoh, who had believed he was a god, had messed with the wrong person. (many people still think this today → Beware!)
Well, actually had messed with the RIGHT and ONLY GOD!
The God of all gods, the God of the Bible.
There can only be ONE!

Pharaoh should have known, he had already experienced the strong hand of God before when he had to go through the 10 plagues and refused to bow down to God. It had also cost him his first-born son.
He had thought that, as an Egyptian god, he was stronger than the God of the Bible. Sorry - wrong thinking.

„And the Egyptians pursued and went after them
into the midst of the sea,
all Pharaoh's horses, his chariots, and his horsemen.
Now it came to pass, in the morning watch,
that the LORD looked down upon the army of the Egyptians
through the pillar of fire and cloud,
and He troubled the army of the Egyptians.
And He took off their chariot wheels,
so that they drove them with difficulty;
and the Egyptians said:
Let us flee from the face of Israel,
for the LORD fights for them against the Egyptians. ...

... Then the LORD said to Moses:
Stretch out your hand over the sea,
that the waters may come back upon the Egyptians,
on their chariots, and on their horsemen.
And Moses stretched out his hand over the sea;
and when the morning appeared,
the sea returned to its full depth,
while the Egyptians were fleeing into it.
So the LORD overthrew the Egyptians in the midst of the sea.
Then the waters returned and covered the chariots,
the horsemen, and all the army of Pharaoh
that came into the sea after them.
Not so much as one of them remained. "
Exodus 14 / 23 – 28

He would rather not have played God or basked in this arrogance. Pride often comes at a high price.

Unfortunately, there are still plenty of them today.

Recently, our daily newspaper published information and an invitation to a special "church service". The invitation came from the Protestant University Student Church in Bamberg and the CSD - Bamberg. (= Christopher Street Day)

To a queer*, Christian-Jewish service.
The stated motto was, hold on tight:

"God is we, God is queer"

Do you still have any words?
I read it three times to make sure I'd seen correctly. I had.
(text source: daily newspaper Fränkischer Tag, 17.07.2024)
Oh Jesus! What blindness. They have never really got to know God and Jesus. They refer to themselves as THE God. "We are God". What presumption and error.

Pharaoh says hello!

Or remember the Olympic opening ceremony on 26 July 2024 in Paris. (text source: numerous media TV, Internet, print)
It was also interesting to see how they portrayed and saw themselves. Was it a reflection of the global sporting community? What message did they want to convey? For some it was "art", for others "perversion", "celebrated ancient Greek myths - performance" or "blasphemy", or something else. You can interpret it however you like. Everyone is free to do so. Thank God. We live in a world of artistic freedom and freedom of opinion. And that's why I can only say for myself, with the spiritual view that I have and believe:
Pharaoh says hello!

By the way - Expensive start to the Summer Games: The spectacular (! - ??) or strange (! - ??) Olympic opening ceremony in Paris cost around 100 million euros. This is according to budget documents from the French parliament, quoted by French media on Thursday (24 October 2024).

We must and can only pray for them, that they may come to the knowledge of the truth and see Jesus and the God of the Bible. And try to tell them about Jesus.
It is still a time of grace!

The apostle Paul puts it this way:

> *„Therefore I exhort first of all that supplications,*
> *prayers, intercessions, and giving of thanks*
> *be made for all men,*
> *for kings and all who are in authority,*
> *that we may lead a quiet and peaceable life*
> *in all godliness and reverence.*
> *For this is good and acceptable in the sight*
> *of God our Saviour, ...*

... who desires all men to be saved
and to come to the knowledge of the truth.
For there is one God and one Mediator
between God and men, the Man Christ Jesus,
who gave Himself a ransom for all,
to be testified in due time,
for which I was appointed a preacher and an apostle
—I am speaking the truth in Christ and not lying—
a teacher of the Gentiles in faith and truth. "
1 Timothy 2 / 1 – 6

Their thinking and lives are truly LGBT o queer. That is why we are praying exactly this biblical passage for the people in Bamberg and the people in charge and show actors in Paris.

„But even if our gospel is veiled,
it is veiled to those who are perishing,
whose minds the god of this age has blinded,
(=Devil, Satan)
who do not believe,
lest the light of the gospel of the glory of Christ,
who is the image of God, should shine on them.
For we do not preach ourselves,
but Christ Jesus the Lord,
and ourselves your bondservants for Jesus' sake. "
2 Corinthians 4 / 3 – 5

Many people think that, like Pharaoh or others, they can define themselves as God and interpret whatever they feel like doing. And even declare it a "service to God" and cheer it on. Oh my goodness.
„Highway to Hell!" - sooner or later.

But there is hope! And that is called →
JESUS CHRIST! The Son of God! The Saviour!

It's better and safer to be on the right side.

Know Jesus and God as described in the Bible.

You are either on the winning side with Jesus or on the losing side with the devil. Life or death. Blessing or curse. World or kingdom of God. Eternal life with Jesus or eternal life in damnation.

It's up to you, the decision is yours.

I'll get round to it - be patient.

But back to our roof. We were still standing there.

On the roof, like Moses, we had stretched out our hand in faith against the danger, the attack, the disaster.

We didn't have a walking rod or sceptre with us at this moment, maybe a jigsaw or hammer, but the hand did it, because we had the name of Jesus.

This is not an old fairy tale, not a "good night story", but the truth, nothing but the truth. And the neighbours became our witnesses.

They came out and asked incredulously what **"that"** was. They had seen everything. Unbelievable!

We explained it to them, proclaimed Jesus to them and invited them to give their lives to Jesus, which they unfortunately did not (yet) do. But they had seen and experienced a miracle of God and had received the explanation for it. They have no more excuses.

„For the wrath of God is revealed from heaven
against all ungodliness and unrighteousness of men,
who suppress the truth in unrighteousness,
because what may be known of God
is manifest in them, for God has shown it to them.
For since the creation of the world,
His invisible attributes are clearly seen,
being understood by the things that are made, ...

... even His eternal power and Godhead,
so that they are without excuse. "
Romans 1 / 18 - 20

Man, every man and woman, and therefore also YOU, because you are also a human being, can perceive God, recognise HIS existence → by HIS works. That is, by what HE has done (for example, creation) and what HE still does in His supernatural power.

Creation is not God. The tree or nature, the sun or anything else is not God.

HE created all this, it is HIS "handmade, handmade; MADE IN HEAVEN," by which we recognise HIS greatness, omnipotence and miraculous work. Ultimately HIM, the

GOD OF THE BIBLE !

And the neighbours said to us: "If you do anything major on the house again, let us know and we'll do some work on our house too, because then we know it will stay dry."

We never did that because they were not or did not want to be under this "rod of the name of Jesus". We didn't want to tempt them to run into disaster.

Whenever we talk about this adventure of faith today, Andra and I, or with others, it seems unreal. BUT WE HAVE EXPERIENCED IT.

We were there in person, live and in colour!
On the roof.

And it totally encouraged us both to find out more about
 – the authority of faith,
 – the authority of the name of Jesus
 – and its practical realisation
to research the Bible, discover it, make it our own, use it and experience tremendous things.

Jesus had shown me that I should write a book about it. And I wrote it.

„With Jesus on patrol"

More about that at the end of this book.

Come and see the works of God;
He is awesome in His doing
toward the sons of men.
the Bible

Highway to Hell

I will come back to the story with the Pharaoh. The "Highway to Hell" and the "Highway to Salvation".

Basically, the "Highway to Salvation" is not a "highway" at all, but a narrow path. But it is the only way to life.
("Highway to Salvation" is a literary pun on my part)

The Bible says there are only these two ways.

> *"Enter by the narrow gate;*
> *for wide is the gate and broad is the way*
> *that leads to destruction,*
> *and there are many who go in by it.*
> *Because narrow is the gate*
> *and difficult is the way which leads to life,*
> *and there are few who find it."*
> Matthew 7 / 13 + 14

The broad, simpler path on which the masses are travelling, today we would say the "main stream", where you can do and leave everything, believe, say and live what and how you want. Right or wrong. Without signposting, without crash barriers, flashing neon signs, you drive or walk criss-cross or queer, it doesn't matter. Yes, of course you can, we live in a free country with guaranteed basic rights. As "Old Fritz" said: "The will of man is his own kingdom of heaven".
(Wikipedia: Frederick II or Frederick the Great (* 24 January 1712 in Berlin; † 17 August 1786 in Potsdam), popularly known as "Old Fritz", was King of Prussia from 1772. / 20.09.2024)

Who brakes - loses. Life is short.
"I want fun - I want fun, I step on the gas - I step on the gas." That used to be the chorus of a song by a singer called Markus from 1982 - "Neue Deutsche Welle" (musicstyle). He

didn't compose it himself, he just sang it. But it hit the zeitgeist. And two months later it was number 1 in the German singles charts.

Fun - whatever the cost, regardless of others. That was the content.

"Highway to Hell" by AC/DC from 1979 is still a hit today. It is played at almost every party, event or other "celebration" and people go crazy for it and join in.

The text speaks for itself, or rather for the devil!

And exactly about the road that leads to hell. A road without borders, no speed limit, no questions ... and the "Highway to Hell" is celebrated in the chorus, hailed as the promised land, where my friends are all already there.

If you're interested in what these guys are saying, what message they are trumpeting to the world millions of times over, then why not take a look on the Internet? You can even have the text translated there if you want. I don't want to reproduce the text here ☹

And there is the narrow way, where there are fewer people on the road and the guard rails are the Word of God.

Man was created by God so that we could have fellowship with HIM and live forever. With HIM. With HIS love and care, like a perfect father with his children.

But man allowed himself to be lied to by the devil and believed him, Mr. Dark.

"You don't need God! The old party pooper! He doesn't begrudge you anything. And anyway, if you disconnect properly, then you're actually God yourself. You decide what is right and wrong, good or bad. So always these oppressive rules - free yourself from them! Live the way you want!"

Man listened to this advice, even though God had warned him against it and the disaster began.

Suddenly man had this sin on his cheek, in his heart, in his spirit. And he couldn't get rid of it by himself.

It's like an incurable disease that leads to death,

a resistant germ in you that will take your life in the long run.

Like the dog poo you stepped in and now can't get off your shoe. No matter what you do - it stinks. No matter how expensive and elegant the shoe is. No matter how much perfume you spray or pour on it - it still stinks.

You can ignore it, deny it, refuse to acknowledge it, talk it down, curse it or try anything else → it stinks. Sin is sin and there is only one remedy for it. But as long as I or you don't make use of this remedy, sin remains on my cheek, in my life, in my spirit - on my shoe.

The human eye for God, HIS love and forgiveness, HIS future with you and me, all that is good and blessed, you can no longer see it.

The devil has got your windscreen all dirty.

(very nice example - I once saw it in a sermon)

And your life sat nav has been hacked and manipulated. You hear and see nothing more of this God and Jesus. You think you are in control and have a clear view. You have been tricked!

You thunder along this "Highway to Hell" without realising that there is no Shindig - Area at the end, but that it simply stops at the edge of the abyss and everyone disappears into this abyss forever. And the stupid thing is, you don't know when it will stop abruptly. There is no more party location. The Bible describes the end of the highway as "HELL".

And that's what it becomes: hell.

This term is also widely used in our everyday language today.

"That was hell" or "we went through hell", for example, are phrases you've probably heard before. They are used to try to explain or convey something that describes a terrifying, horrible, deeply lasting experience or feeling that you don't want to experience again.

Although the person may not even believe in hell, let alone be able to imagine what exactly it is and what it's like.

A place you and I certainly don't want to be!

Unfortunately, you trusted your own life navigation system and other voices, and no one spoke of an abyss. Must be true. The masses are right. Determines what is right and wrong.

That's not true!
There is one voice that says otherwise.
Someone who has defined what is RIGHT or WRONG.
Someone who has the eternal right to define it.
Forever and ever.
Whether we want to hear it or not, believe it or not. It's just there. Always has been. Forever.
And that is the voice of God. "the Navi from Heaven".
HE is calling you and me.

"Watch out - the abyss! End of the highway! Route recalculation! LEAVE THE HIGHWAY! Take the exit."

God has created an exit from this "Highway to Hell". And it is called JESUS:
Not all roads lead to Rome and not all or many lead to heaven. Only one! And his name, as I said, is
JESUS CHRIST.

"We're all, all going to heaven,
because we're so good"!

That's what an old German carnival song makes us believe.

158

Pure lies, deception par excellence, straight from the advertising office of hell, the devil as songwriter.

This "Jesus exit" is totally ingenious. It is practically an invisible, mobile exit that appears when you call for it. It is there at all times, practically travelling alongside you all the time, but you don't see it yet. Maybe you have an inkling or are longing to get off this hellish autobahn.

„A Psalm from David.
LORD, I cry out to You;
Make haste to me!
Give ear to my voice when I cry out to You. "
Psalms 141 / 1

„Behold, the LORD's hand is not shortened,
That it cannot save;
Nor His ear heavy,
That it cannot hear."
Isaiah 59 / 1

„For whoever calls on the name of the LORD
shall be saved."
Romans 10 / 13

Suddenly - there it is, the exit. As if out of nowhere. Jesus – the exit is there and offers you HIMSELF. Jesus hears you immediately when you call out to HIM to get off this damned "Highway to Hell".

You don't have to drive on forever with the realisation that you have to go down, with the fear of falling into the abyss, because you don't know when the abyss is coming. You can't just stop either, there is no emergency lane and those behind

you honk, swear and curse and simply push you on.
"Higher - faster - further → life is bright!"

God saw how man hurtled into the abyss through his sin, with no way out.
And that is why HE sent his son Jesus.
From the heavenly kingdom to the natural world.
From the perfection of God to the imperfection of man.
From clarity to the obfuscation of people.
From a perfect environment to an imperfect one.
From eternity to a temporal, transient world.
From the kingdom of God's peace to a completely chaotic, murderous "Highway to Hell"
Jesus dived into the confused, fallen world to create a way out of it.
HE dived into a lost, dying world to pave a way of salvation, redemption and life.
HE, the Son of God, became the Son of Man so that we could understand and get to know God again.

God has gone all out for you and me, every human being. HE sacrificed and invested HIS best, dearest and most precious things to make this EXIT possible.

So that the fundamental problem of man could be solved for everyone who gets involved with Jesus and trusts him.

HE, Jesus, meets us on this "Highway to Hell" to make a clear announcement.

Jesus was travelling on this "Highway to Hell", HE knows every pothole, every bend, every advertising sign - simply EVERYTHING. We can't fool HIM.

HE even went down the abyss, even though HE knew it was coming. HE didn't have to, but HE did it for us - for me - for you.

He took this "suicide mission" upon Himself.

,,Jesus said to him:
I am the way,
(Way to Salvation)
the truth, and the life.
No one comes to the Father except through Me. "
John 14 / 6

,,All that the Father gives Me will come to Me,
and the one who comes to Me
I will by no means cast out. "
John 6 / 37

GOD made himself understood, in our language, with our means, focussed on our perception.
And HE was very good at it.
HE did it!

,,For God so loved the world
that He gave His only begotten Son,
that whoever believes in Him
should not perish but have everlasting life.
For God did not send His Son into the world
to condemn the world,
but that the world through Him might be saved.
He who believes in Him is not condemned;
but he who does not believe is condemned already,
because he has not believed in the name
of the only begotten Son of God. "
John 3 / 16 - 18

,,For in that He Himself has suffered,
being tempted,
He is able to aid those who are tempted. "
Hebrews 2 / 18

„Let this mind be in you which was also in Christ Jesus,
who, being in the form of God,
did not consider it robbery to be equal with God,
but made Himself of no reputation,
taking the form of a bondservant,
and coming in the likeness of men.
And being found in appearance as a man,
He humbled Himself and became obedient
to the point of death, even the death on the cross.
Therefore God also has highly exalted Him
and given Him the name which is above every name,
that at the name of Jesus every knee should bow,
of those in heaven, and of those on earth,
and of those under the earth,
and that every tongue should confess
that Jesus Christ is Lord,
to the glory of God the Father."
Philippians 2 / 5 – 11

Wow - what a description of the "rescue mission",
the "mission to become human so that we can understand and
be saved again"!!!!
Jesus did not come as Superman, not as an emperor and
general, not as a worldly king or any other kind of leader.

HE came as a simple man. Born in a stable where the
servants normally lived, HE started very low, never made a
fuss, grew up inconspicuously until HE appeared in public at
around 30 years of age and proclaimed and demonstrated HIS
message of salvation. Through HIS death on the cross and
HIS resurrection, HE pushed the door wide open for an
eternity with God,

Have you ever asked yourself where you will spend eternity?

They really do exist. It's not all over with our few years here on earth. Simply gone. Dissolved into atoms. Disappeared into nirvana or something else.

Don't just bury your head in the sand and then the problem or the question is gone. It will pass me by, nothing will happen. NO!
Shall I tell you something? Even with your head in the sand, you will be confronted with exactly that. We've only just read it. Have you forgotten?
A little help:

> „*that at the name of Jesus every knee should bow,*
> *of those in heaven, and of those on earth,*
> ### **and of those under the earth,**
> *(Head in the sand = under the earth?)*
> *and that every tongue should confess*
> *that Jesus Christ is Lord,*
> **to the glory of God the Father.**

Well, the Word of God thinks of everything. Now you can't even stick your head in the sand anymore → Jesus is there too!
Fortunately! Because otherwise we might avoid or ignore the question and the sand fleas would eat our head.

And that is the ultimate question of man and mankind par excellence.
WHERE are you going to spend eternity?

Exactly - WHERE?

I once had to record an accident. It was, of course, part of my job as a policeman.
A young motorcyclist crashed head-on into a car. His "highway" was almost over. He survived "as if by a miracle". The guardian angel had been there. He had another chance.

He was hospitalised with bruises and a swollen knee like a football, but nothing else. Motorbike and car totalled.

And in the hospital, after the accident report, I asked him this question. "Where would you be now if you had died?"

He became a little insecure and initially tried to play down the subject and play it cool. But I didn't let up and kept asking if he knew God and how he felt about HIM. Whether he really knew where he would be when he died.

He then told me honestly that he somehow believed in God up there, that he had been baptised as a baby and that he hoped that would be enough for heaven. After all, that's what the priest had told him and promised him.

He lay there in front of me in the hospital bed, his knee swollen and blue, I felt so sorry for him. The bloke had no idea about eternity, had no real relationship with God and still hoped that it would be enough?

Oh yes, I offered to pray for supernatural healing because the doctors had already told him he would have to stay in hospital for a long time because of his knee. He agreed and I put my hand on the swollen knee and commanded in the name of Jesus:

"Swelling go away,
Knee be healed - in the name of Jesus
and Jesus I ask YOU,
that he can go home after 2 - 3 days"

A prayer against the doctor's prognosis and Jesus had answered it.

The motorcyclist told me on the phone the next morning that the swelling of the knee was completely gone, including the blue colouring of the skin. Everything was normal. The doctors were totally surprised at the morning visit, couldn't explain it, but everything was fine again and ordered him to be discharged home the next day.

Isn't Jesus AWESOME?

But back to the conversation at the bedside. Mamma mia! Had nobody really told him?

That the baptism of a baby has nothing to do with "going to heaven", but nothing at all?

Doesn't he know …

… that only a relationship with Jesus is the ticket?
... that you can't get past Jesus?
... that Jesus loves him infinitely and died for him?
... that Jesus is waiting for a reaction, an invitation?
... that it only works if you accept Jesus into your life
    and ask for forgiveness?
... that you can and should live with Jesus?

I thought about how I could best explain it to him and prayed silently for an idea. And it came!

I had a recently injured person here who had been treated by the emergency doctor and admitted to hospital. He was lucky again (?) (!).

And so I explained it to him my way.
"You know, when you had the accident and were lying there, did it do you any good that you knew there was an emergency doctor? No. This knowledge, even if it's 1000%, won't do you any good. You will bleed to death and die.

Yes, there is an emergency doctor, one who is super - well trained. Who is ready to go into action day and night. Who

165

will do everything possible to help you. Who will put his own life on the line to save yours.

It's not enough to know that there is an emergency doctor. He doesn't come on his own, he has to be called.

He also knows that accidents happen, but he only comes when he is needed.

Have you ever noticed that emergency doctors don't go on patrol, along the lines of: "Let's see if we see a seriously injured person lying around somewhere that we can somehow give a plaster" or "Well - then we'll just injure one ourselves so that we can treat him and look good".

Hey, that doesn't exist.

Jesus is waiting for an invitation from you. HE is ready to save, liberate and restore you. But HE is waiting for your own, willing decision! Do you want to invite Jesus? Do you want to entrust and hand over your life to Him? Do you want to trust Him? Do you want to take the "JESUS exit"?

He had understood this example and these questions. That fully met his situation. I told him what the Bible says about it.

> *„ Call upon Me in the day of trouble;*
> *I will deliver you,*
> *and you shall glorify Me. "*
> Psalms 50 / 15

Somehow you can't get anywhere in life without this passage from the Bible.

Other biblical passages illustrate this as follows:

*"for the Son of Man has come
to seek and to save that which was lost."*
Luke 19 / 10

"But as many as received Him (Jesus)
(in their lives, under HIS direction),
to them He gave the right
(power, authority)
*to become children of God,
to those who believe in His name."*
John 1 / 12

And so we prayed together and he gave his life to Jesus, asked for forgiveness of his sin and received his salvation and his new birth there on his sickbed.
Now he was able to answer the question about eternity with joy, because certainty had come into his mind and heart through the Holy Spirit.
Hallelujah!!!!

You've read this far and you might be thinking: That's not possible! I've never heard or seen anything like that. I only know God or Jesus from religion lessons and it was boring. My grandma told me something about it, but that wasn't really exciting either. I had to go to church as a child and it was totally irritating. This Jesus and the whole faith thing is alien to life, wrong, antiquated and quite hypocritical.

You may be partly right because **you** may have had profoundly negative experiences in the past.

If you have been disappointed in the name of God or in the name of Jesus, by people who were supposed to tell you about love and the offer of salvation, but instead abused you mentally, physically or spiritually, then I am totally sorry for you. Honestly.

But it's not God's fault!
HE will never let you down or abuse you. This is what people have done to you who allow themselves to be led by Satan, who are themselves in demonic dependence. I don't care what their name is, what ecclesiastical position they have or had or what denomination they belong to. It was abysmal sin that led to you being misinformed, seeing and experiencing repulsive examples and no longer wanting to know anything about Jesus. They slammed the door to eternity shut for you instead of opening it.
This is the handwriting of Mr Abominable - the devil!

And I apologise to you at this point for all those who set you a bad example, who took you away from God and his Son Jesus instead of bringing you to Jesus.
They have lied to you, have consciously lied to you or have been lied to themselves, have led you astray, into unbelief, rejection, rebellion, confusion and 'false security'.

Do you know what Jesus says about these people, these "false leaders or people"?

„It would be better for him
if a millstone were hung around his neck,
and he were thrown into the sea,
than that he should offend one of these little ones. "
Luke 17 / 2

This applies equally to men and women,
who become guilty of you
and you don't get to know Jesus or get to know him wrongly
because of this

Jesus, the Son of God, lives and HE loves you and stretches out HIS hand to you. HE wants to save you and forgive your sin. The sin is not primarily what you have or have not done, it is the sin of not believing in the name of Jesus.
(Gospel of John chapter 16, verse 9, there it is, if you want to read it).
And that stands between God and you and prevents you from going to heaven one day.

It is not enough to have heard about Jesus and then HE will do it. Jesus is waiting for your invitation so that HE can save you. (Think of the emergency doctor)

He wants to put the exit at your feet as quickly as you allow. Everything you need is already ready. Perhaps no one has ever told you this before. Jesus purchased redemption, the forgiveness of (your) sins and a complete restoration with his blood and life on the cross. All you have to do is claim it for yourself. Consciously say "yes" and believe. That´s it!

The blood of Jesus is the only effective "remedy" to get rid of stinking sin. The only one. The blood of Jesus. For you and me.
No grass will grow over it, even the time that passes won't change anything. Sin can only be eradicated by the BLOOD OF JESUS and by NOTHING else.

„...having wiped out
the handwriting of requirements that was against us,
which was contrary to us.
And He has taken it out of the way,
having nailed it to the cross."
Colossians 2 / 14

„But if we walk in the light as He is in the light,
we have fellowship with one another,
and the blood of Jesus Christ His Son
cleanses us from all sin. "

"If we confess our sins,
He is faithful and just to forgive us our sins
and to cleanse us from all unrighteousness. "
1 John 1 / 7 + 9

Invite Jesus
to come into your life,
get to know HIM
and be your Lord.

You will see that Jesus is different from what you may have been told.

A life without Jesus is boring, pointless, without a future. People without Jesus have no idea what freedom, peace, joy, enthusiasm, strength and excitement life here on earth can have. And beyond that, a life in eternity with Jesus.

Where will you spend eternity? What if there is something to life after death? You should have or receive an answer to these existential questions of life. Just like the motorcyclist.
In our everyday lives, we make provisions for everything possible or impossible. But many fail to make provision for eternity with the one who is responsible for it. Jesus! HE is our "life insurance" in the most literal sense, and HE guarantees it with HIS word if we accept HIM and don't let go again.

Jesus is God's answer to our lostness. And one day you will not be able to avoid this decision. At the latest when you stand before HIM, but then it is too late to make a decision.

By then everything has to be wrapped up. That's why prayers for the deceased are no longer of any use. It is over. Sorry! †

Either you knew Jesus and accepted HIM into your life and lived with HIM or you did not.
There is no subsequent possibility. No second life with reincarnation and all that. Anyone who tells you that is either lying to you or doesn't know any better.

Decide now, here and now, to live with Jesus and give your life to Jesus. Don't wait for a later or better time. There is none. What counts is NOW, because it can suddenly be too late. I have seen many accidental deaths where people were torn from this life to eternity from one minute to the next and suddenly stood before God the Creator and their judge. They may have thought they still had time to answer this question. Rumble to an end. Too late! Gone. Highway over, chance missed, eternity with Jesus gambled away. † ☹

I invite you to a new life with Jesus;
to experience HIS love, strength and forgiveness and that HE may take care of your needs and illnesses.
Trust in HIM!
And you will experience miracles.
Miracles of salvation, deliverance, forgiveness, healing.
Miracles of divine help in your life.
Miracles are part of it.
100 percent!
This whole salvation process is a miracle!

Are you wondering how to do this?
Simply speak to Jesus!
You don't have to change beforehand, become better or anything like that. That's nonsense, that's religious drivel. Speak to HIM, simply in the state and situation you are in at the moment. In your own words, however stammered they

may be. Jesus understands you. He even hears the silent cry for help from your heart.

If someone needs to be rescued from the mud hole they're stuck in because otherwise they'll be swallowed up, you don't say to them beforehand: "You can only be rescued when you're showered, cleanly dressed and your hair is in place." That's nonsense. The same goes for faith. No matter where you are - Jesus is waiting for you and will hear you.

Invite him, accept Jesus into your life. Believe and confess it.

The Bible says:

> *„But as many as received Him,* (Jesus)
> (into their lives, under HIS direction),
> *to them He gave the right*
> (power, authority)
> *to become children of God,*
> *to those who believe in His name. "*
> John 1 / 12
> (the scripture is so important, that's why I'm repeating it here)

> *„For with the heart one believes unto righteousness,*
> *and with the mouth confession is made unto salvation. "*
> Romans 10 / 10

It's not difficult. But nobody can make this decision for you. Not your parents, not your grandma, certainly not any church, whatever it is called and whatever it has promised you. Only you and Jesus. Only you two can make it clear.

Jesus will never force you, but you should think about it, because things can quickly turn out very differently.

Pray to Jesus now, in the place where you have just read it,

172

and commit your life into the hands of the most wonderful, loving, powerful and gracious Lord the world has ever seen or will ever see and you will experience HIM ...

Jesus Christ

The following prayer is a little help, if you don't know how to pray for salvation.

Prayer for salvation

If you want to know Jesus and you know that you need forgiveness and salvation, I invite you to pray the following prayer aloud, earnestly and with confidence:

Lord Jesus Christ,
I believe and confess with all my heart
that You are the Son of God
and came to earth to redeem me.
You died on the cross for my sake
and took my sin upon Yourself
so that I can be free.
You rose from the dead and are alive.
I confess my sins to you.
I ask You to forgive me
and wash me clean through Your blood.
I receive You into my life,
and confess:
YOU alone are my Saviour and Lord!
To all other powers,
to which I had opened myself
must disappear from my life!
In Jesus' name.

Holy Spirit,
please fill me with the power of God,
so thatI can grow in faith
and see more and more of Jesus
and understand the word of God.
I want to experience your marvellous power.
Thank you Jesus!

What comes next?

Congratulations! If you have just said the prayer to Jesus in earnest, then you are off the "Highway to Hell" - you are now a child of God! You are on the "Way to Salvation". Welcome to the family of God!

You have embarked on a new path with Jesus at your side. The Bible explains it as a "new birth". As I said, this has nothing at all to do with reincarnation. You are not coming back to earth in any form of life. You are a new creature from the Spirit of God. Not outwardly, but spiritually something marvellous has happened. The greatest miracle that a human being can experience.

No matter whether you felt something special or not. Salvation is ultimately not a feeling, but a fact of faith. Feelings can be.
Relief, peace, joy, warmth, acceptance and much more. But please don't make it dependent on a feeling. The Bible says that it is when we sincerely receive Jesus and that's it. Full stop. That's it. Enough said! Hallelujah.

> *„Therefore, if anyone is in Christ,*
> *he is a new creation;*
> *old things have passed away;*
> *behold, all things have become new.“*
> 2 Corinthians 5 / 17

You are now part of the winning team. The power of the devil has been broken in your life.

Now your new life in Jesus Christ should grow and become strong, so that the things you do that are not right will also disappear from your life.

Just as a newborn baby needs care, protection and support as it grows and learns, so do you in your faith. You need people who know and follow Jesus. People who can show and explain to you how you can live and talk with Jesus. By the way, this is called PRAYING. Not necessarily pre-formulated prayers, but just what is on your heart.

Get yourself a Bible. Read it every day, preferably starting with the New Testament, for example in the Gospel of John, because it gives a great description of who Jesus is and what He did and said. You can trust HIM and His word. You will see that it is more exciting than you think.

There are many good Bible translations, including some in smooth, modern English. You have to see what you get on with best.

You need a lively church where you feel at home. A church with people who love Jesus and are enthusiastic about HIM and share what HE has just done again. Who know the God of miracles and power.

Where the Holy Spirit has the freedom to perform miracles. Where people tell how Jesus actively and supernaturally intervened. Have a look at their website to see if you can find reports of healings, interventions by God, answers to prayer or other miracles. If yes - have a look around, if no – well. Then keep searching and ask Jesus to show you the right place.

Where you and others are prayed for personally, where healing, release and restoration are normal. Where you can use your talents and gifts and you can grow. There are more churches and groups than you think.

The Apostle Paul admonished Christians that faith must stand on the visible connection between the clear word of God and the effective power.

„And my speech and my preaching
were not with persuasive words of human wisdom,
but in demonstration of the Spirit and of power,
that your faith should not be in the wisdom of men
but in the power of God."
1 Corinthians 2 / 4 + 5

"But I will come to you shortly,
if the Lord wills, and I will know,
not the word of those who are puffed up,
but the power.
For the kingdom of God
is not in word
but in power. "
1 Corinthians 4 / 20

Not just clever words without a visible demonstration of God's power. If they want to make you believe that these things no longer exist today or that you can no longer see the word of God as it is written in the Bible, beware of them. They deny the power of God and you would not be able to grow and really experience Jesus.

"having a form of godliness
but denying its power.
And from such people turn away!"
2 Timothy 3 / 5

Just google your city. Type in:
"Jesus" - "Holy Spirit" - "Healing" - "Miracle" .

Then take a look at their websites to see if there is any life in them. Have a look there and get an idea of the group and their service. You will find the right place. Jesus will guide you.

But please find a church or group. It is vital. The Bible does not recognise a Christian without a church. That is spiritual death and the beginning of a lot of confusion. There are some who think they don't need a living church. Don't listen to them.

If you ever come to Bamberg / Germany, I would be delighted to welcome you to the Jesus Gemeinde Bamberg. (www.jesus-gemeinde.de)

Do you know that your life is now in the hands and care of Jesus? He now has your permission to put things in order in your life and to help you. And to bring you into this "WONDER - FULL" kingdom of God.

You will see and experience it! Faith in Jesus is practical.

Welcome to the "Way to Salvation"

We pray for you and for every reader of this book. Jesus bless you!

(Note: In the chapter you just read, I took passages from my first two books and reused them here)

We would like to take you travelling with us again. Let's go to Mexico and Egypt. Pack your swimming trunks ..., binoculars, sun cream and your Bible. Off to the ancient civilisations, the pyramids, sites of human history and of Günther and Andra. Excitement, thrills and adventure await - what are we waiting for?
Here are two more "delicacies", "tasty titbits".

Total lost

Years ago we flew to Mexico on holiday. For four weeks, just the flight! The rest of the country on our own. We've always been brave. We spoke almost no Spanish, quite good English and we had been told that you could get by with it anywhere in the world.
We will see – said the blind man.

Travelling around the country, exploring everything on our own, without the internet - that didn't exist back then - (yes, we're that old!) a printed travel guide in our pockets. Travel preparations completed at home. We knew where we wanted to go and what we wanted to see.

Put the journey, including the planning, in God's hands and gooooooooooo!

> *„Commit your way to the LORD,*
> *Trust also in Him,*
> *And He shall bring it to pass. "*
> Psalms 37 / 5

> *„Commit your works to the LORD,*
> *And your thoughts will be established. "*
> Proverbs 16 / 3

Mexico City, the old Aztec capital "Tenochtitlan" from the 13th century, Templo Mayor, the Pyramid of the Sun and the Pyramid of the Moon, the water gardens and the old canals, the historic centre and the busy life. A dream. Only the smog was a nightmare. After a short time you had a nosebleed, the air was so corrosive.
Let's run away!

We only travelled around the country on "local buses", not air-conditioned tourist buses. It's much more interesting, you get around more, the chickens run around your legs (no idea how the various owners recognised and caught them when they got off), we travelled during the day - you see something, and we travelled at night - you don't need a hotel.

Off to the bus terminal and next stop the old, famous jet-set city of Acapulco.
While we were there, we didn't want to miss out on the world-famous rock jumpers. It's death-defying! It's a very narrow rocky bay into which the Pacific waves crash.

One side of the bay is steep, so the jumpers climb the 40 metres up the cliff "La Quebrada" barefoot, stand there, watch the waves, calculate their own flight time and the wave length and height and then jump headfirst into this narrow bay, hoping that they won't hit the cliff or be pushed against it by the wind. Some have already lost their lives during these daring jumps.

On the other side of the cliff, we sat safely and comfortably in the café and watched the spectacle. We asked ourselves why they were doing this, it was actually crazy.

But well, we were kind of crazy to watch something like that. But that's life, it builds up. They jump like crazy so that spectators come, are amazed, applaud them, tip them, they climb back up the cliff with their chests swelling with pride.

Another jump, another round of applause, another tip.

Enough sightseeing, onwards by bus to Taxco, a silver mining town,Fantastic food, beautiful city centre, up the mountain in an old VW Beetle taxi. An adventure. You never know if you'll live to see the next day. But Jesus is with us. ☹

And back to the Pacific coast to Puerto Escondido ... for a swim with pelicans!

Mamma Mia – I tell you, that's really something special. You're swimming and suddenly a huge pelican swoops in from a lofty height 30 cm next to you, having seen a fish swimming around your feet, and takes it. Actually, you should swim with a steel helmet, but then you'll get drowned.

But now you also know how important the helmet of salvation is. (Ephesians 6 / 17) I believe it also helps against pelicans! ☺

But it was exciting! Wham - another one. They flew and dived en masse. We had experienced it → survived it. ☺

Beat it! Oaxaca, Chichen Itzá, many ruins of the ancient Mayas, we wanted to go down to the Yucatan Peninsula to Cancun and then take the plane back to Mexico City, from there back to Germany.

Wikipedia: (29.05.2024)
Chichén Itzá is one of the most important ruins on the Mexican peninsula of Yucatán. It is located around 120 kilometres east of Mérida in the state of Yucatán. Its ruins date back to the late Mayan period. Covering an area of 1547 hectares, Chichén Itzá is one of the most extensive archaeological sites in Yucatán. The centre is occupied by numerous monumental representative buildings with a religious and political background, from which a large, largely preserved step pyramid stands out. There are ruins of upper-class houses in the immediate vicinity. Chichén Itzá was declared a World Heritage Site by UNESCO in 1988.

(Just for a little informacion).

The trip was spectacular, we were thrilled, everything went like clockwork, the travel guide (i.e. the little booklet) lived up to its name, everything fitted, was as described, always a hit.

And we knew and felt: Jesus was with us.

According to Psalm 37 / 5 (Do you remember? "Commit your way to the Lord, ...)

These ancient buildings, temples, human sacrifices - ancient witnesses to murderous efforts just to appease their gods and gain favour. What an effort, what a difference to the God of the Bible. God has done everything, HE has made the sacrifice for the forgiveness of sin through Jesus, all we have to do now is accept it.

We could literally see the ancient Mayans running around in the ruins, seeking salvation and redemption. And above the temples and sacrificial altars, the demonic princes shouting to the ancient Mayans: "That's not enough - more blood, more human hearts torn out, more, more ... sacrifices!"

In the guidebook we read that there was a railway station on our route, in an oil-mining village, and from there it would be a comfortable train journey of several hours to Merida, in the direction of Yucatan.

Unfortunately, I can't remember the name of the oil diggers' village.

Well, that's something new, we thought, and travelled by bus to this small settlement on the Pacific coast.

The bus terminal was on the edge of town, it was brand new, a large area with parking bays for the buses, new paving slabs as far as the eye could see. Someone had spent a lot of money on it. He was obviously expecting a lot of buses. Lots and lots of buses. But in the end it was just a large, bare and lonely area.

Our bus was the only one!

We got off the → the bus escaped immediately, as if stung by a tarantula. The driver was probably scared of the "banditos". You know: paunched, dirty, big moustache, huge sombrero, bandoleers crossed over his chest, bloodthirsty, ... cinema cliché.

So off we went with our suitcases to the railway station, which was in the centre of town. You know your way around, you have a travel guide.

Past many small, empty houses, all deserted, desolate, bleak, oppressive.
Something was wrong here!
The travel guide spoke of a train connection, but no one even lives here.
Raid? Indians? All massacred? Plague? Aliens? Extinct?

Stop there! A Mexican! But he was totally drunk, covered in his huge sombrero, half on the road, half on the pavement.
Nothing again. Unresponsive.
(Incidentally, this was a common sight we saw on our trip - it was sad)

Dry bushes rolled across the streets in the wind, it was like in the old westerns. Django against Manolito! And the bushes. The only thing missing was the right music. "Play me the song of death" or something.

By the way, these dry bush balls are officially called

"tumbleweeds or Ruthenian saltwort".

And the botanists or Western fans among you know that they are called "Salsola tragus" in Latin. Of course - how else! Well, you'll learn something for life here. You'll be able to shine the next time you're asked about it.

But who asks about that ☺ !
Then finally the railway station! Hallelujah!
Ooppps! Well, it had seen better days. No matter.

The entrance door to the station lobby was like a saloon. Two small swinging doors. Oh right - we're in Mexico, live and in colour. No saloon → railway station! → Estación! (in original spanish) The scenery in front of us would have done honour to any Hollywood western.

We went through the swinging doors - squeak → swing → squeeeeak → swing → squeeeeak → swing → we are in it.
We are there, but alone. Everything deserted, dilapidated, just us and the dry bushes, these "tumbleweeds" rolling by. In the middle of the draughty station concourse. Or should we say "stationweeds"?
And we stand there lost with our two suitcases.

We suddenly had a total, final revelation:

WE ARE LOST!
WIR SIND VERLOREN!

Horror, panic and helplessness spread. We cried out to Jesus for help. "Lord Jesus, we had entrusted everything to you. And now this! We are lost here! Have you abandoned us?"

The word from Psalm 50 reached our thoughts, our hearts. Verse 15 struck us to the core and pulled us out of our beginning frustration:

> *„and call upon me in the day of trouble,*
> *and I will save you,*
> *and you shall praise me!. "*

Do you remember it? We already had the verse in connection

with the "Highway to Hell"

This was written for us, the old psalm writer Asaf must have known thousands of years ago that we would one day be stranded in Mexico. Perhaps he had experienced something similar? Alone in the desert in a deserted caravanserai* and not one camel in sight? Only tumbleweeds? And that's why he wrote?
Anyway - praise the Lord for that.

That is one of the great secrets of the Bible, the Word of God: despite being 4000 or more years old, it is still up to date, still spot on. It is God's living word that you can rely on. It works, brings things about or changes things.

(Jesus)
„Heaven and earth will pass away,
but My words will by no means pass away. "
Matthew 24 / 35

Let's go back to Psalm 50.
Verse 15 is also lovingly called
"the telephone number of God":

☎: 50 – 15

„Call on me and I (God) will save you..."

And that's what we did. We called, immediately, without a phone, free of charge, but not for nothing.
(remember, there was no internet or Google or smartphones - oh how relaxed life was!)

„Jesus - help us, we're lost here!"

Our phone connection was prayer.
We already had 5G back then, oh what → 6G!
"Gebet, Glaube, Gewißheit, Gott, Geist Gottes, Gottes Wort!"
(Prayer, faith, certainty, God, Spirit of God, Word of God)
Unfortunately, this play on words doesn't work in English. All
these words begin in German with -G-.
6G!

Manno, we were ahead of our time! And we still have 6G.
The contract keeps renewing for as long as we want. Free of
charge! Forever!
And imagine that God was actually at the other end!

We looked outside.

A taxi!
    A taxi indeed!
        Made of sheet metal, tyres and fuel!
          With a driiiiiver!
            With a living cabbie! (=taxista)

For us!

("taxista" is the Spanish word for the taxi driver. I will use
more Spanish words on the next pages, because we are in
Mexico at the moment. Ok? Comprende? Thanks! Gracias!
Todo bien! Claro!!) ☺

God had answered promptly. I have no idea where the rust
bucket suddenly came from.

> *,,...be strong and of good courage, and do it;*
> *do not fear nor be dismayed,*
> *for the LORD God—my God—will be with you.*
> *He will not leave you nor forsake you, ..."*
> 1 Chronicles 28 / 20

Well, who says so!

We were the only passengers. Of course, there was nobody else there. Far and wide.
Just the two of us and the taxista. We wouldn't let him go now. He could drive us back to civilisation.

With our two bits of Spanish, we tried to find out what was going on here and when the next train to Merida was leaving. (because he didn't speak English, my goodness - you can get by with English anywhere in the world. Not here, in the middle of the Mexican western with the tumbleweeds!)

After a long back and forth, German - English - Spanish, hands and feet → the sobering result: There is no train at all, the station has been closed for years. The guide hadn't known and had sent us offside. Manno – Mann!

"The bus station!" The saving and, above all, cheaper idea. Maybe there's a bus that will take us away from here. After all, we have arrived also.

The taxista didn't even want to take us to the bus station, the distance was too short for him, he probably sensed the ride of his life and wanted to retire with our fare. Sombrero - tequila - chicas - monetas and all that.
Nope - bus station! Vamos! Anderle! Let´s go!

He drove us there, annoyed because he saw his retirement disappear, demanded a utopian fare for one or two kilometres, which of course we didn't pay. I gave him a few pesos, he wanted more, I stood firm. I didn't want to buy the whole of Mexico. Let him get his Mexican banditos colleagues with their bandoliers crossed over their chests. I didn't care. After all, I was the sheriff and I wasn't afraid! What's a few banditos?

Suddenly he jumped on his horse - er, into his taxi - and sped off.

We were alone again and lost!
All alone in the wide area, visible from all sides. Not even a street dog. Exasperating.

So call again! The 50 - 15!
We knew the number by heart. It even works without an international dialling code, which you usually don't know anyway.

„Jesus! Heeeelp!"

Our eyes fell on the ticket office in the centre of the square. It was worth a try. Probably not occupied. No one, no bus, no porter. Why would there be?

I went in, it said "Tickets - Billetes" in big letters and what a miracle. There was a porter behind his desk! Thank you Jesus.

The "Mex - Man" was a colossus of a man, tall, fat, huge moustache, the only thing missing was the sombrero. But he was sitting in the shade. And in a proud porter's uniform.
He smelt of cheap Mezcal (a simple version of Tequila) and was asleep.
Yes, you read that right. He slept soundly, snoring like a walrus.

I spoke to him - nothing - nada!
I shouted at him - nothing - nada!
I shook him - nothing - nada!
I punched him - nothing - nada!

He was asleep. As if dead. But the snoring showed that he was still alive. Dead people don't snore, they're just dead and silent. Honestly - I learnt that at school. And that's logical for once.

There was also no timetable or other information at the counter.

What good is a porter if he can't make it?

Resigned, I went back out to Andra. We sat on a bench next to our suitcases.

"What are we doing now?"
"We'll do what we always do – give a call!"

(50 - 15, without dialling code!)
"Lord Jesus - help!
We are lost again.
Please send someone to us,
who can at least speak a bit of English
and help us further."

We sat on the bench and looked around the whole area in silence.

Suddenly a hippie came out from behind the "Billetes Office". I have no idea how he got there. We hadn't seen anyone walking across the square. Maybe he had been sleeping in the shade. No matter.

About 25 to 30 years old, slim, long Rasta hair, Hawaiian shirt, frayed jeans, you wouldn't trust him with your suitcase in Mexico either. That was my first thought, but then I somehow got the impression that his face had a European flavour and that you could probably trust him. First impressions are sometimes deceptive. Maybe it's not a bad idea to just talk to him. We don't have to give him our suitcases. Hold on to your wallet! And besides, we had no other choice.

He came up to us and I spoke to him in English.
„Excuse me Sir, can you help us?"

I was just about to continue with my school English when he looked at me kindly, grinned and said to me: "Why do you speak English, you're from Germany. We can speak German."

We were left breathless. Totally floored. There's no such thing!
He speaks German! Sapperlot*! The bighit!

And that is how our God is.
We thought we were asking God for someone who spoke a little English. That was as far as our logic, or faith, went.
God had probably smiled about it and sent us something better.

> „Now to Him who is able to do exceedingly abundantly
> above all that we ask or think,
> according to the power that works in us,"
> Ephesians 3 / 20

HEY - You can trust God for more than you think. If I'm already empty-handed, then HE still has enough trump cards up his sleeve.

We talked and told him about our plight and that we wanted to take the bus back to Oaxaca.

"Wait a minute, we're almost there!" replied our German-Mexican hippie.

He went into the porter's cabin and I could watch him from outside.

The hippie whispered something in the Mex's ear, which seemed completely pointless after my attempts to wake him up.

Mex - Man woke up immediately, shot up from his resting position as if he had heard the trumpets of Jericho. He immediately started sweating.

Our helper grabbed the porter by the collar, pulled him over the counter towards him and demanded
,, Dos billetes a Oaxaca – pero rápido!"
(Two tickets to Oaxaca, but quickly)

The porter got busy, gave the hippie two tickets and quoted the price, the sweat intensified.

Our hippie friend called the price to me outside, I took out a banknote and handed it to him.

Our "saviour" came out with tickets and change, gave it to me and said:

"Stay here at the bus platform, bus no. 5 will be here in 10 minutes and will take you directly to Oaxaca."

I looked at my watch: 2.50 pm. Overjoyed, I pocketed the change and turned round briefly to Andra to give her the bus tickets. That took maybe 10 seconds - at most.

I turned round again to thank our hippie and ask how we could do something good for him.

HE WAS GONE!
Simply gone! Simply disappeared! As if vanished into thin air. There was no sign of him for miles around, not even behind the "Billetes", not even inside. I looked, the Mex was already sawing up whole imaginary forests again.(snoring)

A panoramic view of the square, which can be seen from afar - nothing to be seen. Not a soul to be seen.

It slowly dawned on us what and who God had sent us:

An ANGEL

Dressed up as a hippie! So that we are not frightened. Most of the time, the angels in the Bible had to tell people first when they met them:

„Don´t be afraid!"

„Now there were in the same country
shepherds living out in the fields,
keeping watch over their flock by night.
And behold, an angel of the Lord stood before them,
and the glory of the Lord shone around them,
and they were greatly afraid.
Then the angel said to them:
Do not be afraid,
for behold, I bring you good tidings of great joy
which will be to all people.
For there is born to you this day in the city of David
a Savior, who is Christ the Lord."
Luke 2 / 8 – 11

This is just one of many places where angels come and first say: "Do not be afraid"

Angels are mighty beings, created by God, not these small, chubby, dreamy-looking, kitschy, curly-haired children - little angels with their big bums sticking out.
They are puttoes!

Internet:
The idea that these childlike angels bestow love and other pleasant feelings has also become established in the Christian religion over the centuries, so that puttoes have been used in the church architecture of many epochs as givers of happiness and messengers sent from heaven.
(text source:) Floristik21 / 31.05.2024)

What a pity, that is such a belittling of the mighty servants and messengers of God. I don't know how you see it with the angels, so let's take a little excursion into the Word of God. Angels appear from beginning to end. Always on behalf of God. HE alone is the chief of the angels. Even Jesus did not command the angels during his time on earth, but left it to HIS Father. For example:

> *„Or do you think*
> **that I cannot now pray to My Father,**
> *and He will provide Me*
> *with more than twelve legions of angels? "*
> Matthew 26 / 53

Jesus was the Son of Man on Earth, and according to his own statement, he could have prayed to his Father to request help from 12 legions of angels.

HE, as Jesus, did not command the angels to come. HE also did not say,
"If I wanted to, I could command the 12 legions of angels to my aid."
HE was referring to the occupying Roman power at that time.

NO – HE left it to the Father – the LORD OF HOSTS.
The same applies to us: we can ask our Father in heaven for the service of the angels if HE does not already do so of HIS own accord.
Thank you God for this tremendous support.

By the way: 1 legion of Roman soldiers was a whole bunch of people back then! And Jesus spoke of 12 legions.
Mamma Mia!

Wikipedia: (21.09.2024)
A Roman legion (from the Latin legio, from legere "to read" in the sense of "to select", "to choose") was an independently operating military unit in the Roman Empire, usually consisting of 3,000 to 6,000 heavy infantry soldiers and a small detachment of about 120 legion cavalry.

You can imagine what would have happened if there had suddenly been about 70,000 angels there.

They are sent by God to proclaim the plan of God, to help, to accompany, to protect, to punish and much more.
But always as mighty ministering spirits. Strong, unconquerable, endowed with the resources of heaven.
Anything else would not do justice to the almighty God, the ruler of heaven and earth. And certainly not PUTTOES! ☹

Here is a small selection of Bible scriptures:

„Are they not all ministering spirits
sent forth to minister for those
who will inherit salvation? ?“
Hebrews 1 / 14

to serve those who shall receive salvation.
That's you and me. We are meant to be saved according to God's will, if we recognise it and want it. Angels at our side, whether you see them or not, hippies or someone else, perceptible as a man or a woman, it doesn't matter. Servants of God for you and me.

„Behold, I send an Angel before you
to keep you in the way
and to bring you into the place which I have prepared. “
Exodus 23 / 20

„The angel of the LORD *encamps all around those*
who fear Him, And delivers them. "
Psalms 34 / 7

„Bless the LORD, *you His angels,*
Who excel in strength, who do His word,
Heeding the voice of His word.
Bless the LORD, *all you His hosts,*
You ministers of His, who do His pleasure. "
Psalms 103 / 20 + 21

„Then the devil left Him, and behold,
angels came and ministered to Him. "
(After Jesus had been tempted in the wilderness)
Matthew 4 / 11

„Do not forget to entertain strangers,
for by so doing some have unwittingly entertained angels. "
Hebrews 13 / 2
(I wonder what the guests looked like?)

These are a few descriptions of angels and their tasks. And
the Bible has many more. It is impossible to imagine God's
environment without them.

And it wasn't in the lives of the early Christians either. Just
read the book of Acts, for example.

And here we were, having met an angel in person and talked
to him. Now we also knew why he knew that we were from
Germany. He could have told us our home address and name,
but then we would probably have fainted and would still be
lying there today. Without the sombrero.

The last confirmation came by bus.

According to Mister Hippie-Angel, the bus should arrive in 10 minutes, number 5.

During our travels, we had never seen a punctual bus, let alone one with a number. Most of the time, it had some destination written on it, and you had to ask.
Our faith has already been severely tested.

And lo and behold, the number 5 bus arrived at our platform right on time!
Another miracle that we hadn't expected. But it was there, in the form of bus no. 5!
Actually, there were several miracles:
Miracle 1: There actually was a bus
Miracle 2: Right on time
Miracle 3: It actually had a number: 5
Miracle 4: It came to "our" platform
Miracle 5: It saved us and dropped us off in Oaxaca

Some things are just too crazy for words!
We don't even know how many angels we have met on the most diverse occasions without recognising them.
One day in heaven, some angels will surely ask us: "Do you still recognise us?"
And then we: "Uhh – sorry? Not that we know of."
And then they will tell us the story of our encounters. It will certainly be exciting. We are looking forward to it.

We remembered another incident that took place two or three years before our trip to Mexico. We were in Alexandria, Egypt.

We had just left the hotel to go on a full day of sightseeing. We had prayed, put the day in God's hands, asked for HIS protection and guidance, amen – all good.

An Egyptian was standing in front of the hotel who had apparently been waiting just for us. He approached us directly and said:
"I'm your city guide for today!" It wasn't (!) a question. It was a statement.
Andra and I looked at each other. There were a lot of tourists in the hotel, and they were all swarming out.

"You must have us mixed up with someone else, we didn't order a city guide."

"But I'm here for you today. I'm not taking any money, please just pay for the tickets for me."
Well – we thought, it's peanuts, it won't make us poor. We won't get rid of the guy anyway.

Unfortunately, this is often how we feel: we pray and ask for something from God and then we don't really expect a prompt answer, just because it may look different from what we think or don't think at all. Do you sometimes feel the same way? Then welcome to the learners' club!

Often we pray and then we make serious suggestions to God about how HE could help us in the best way. Isn't that crazy?

We left him there and went towards the tram stop to travel to our first destination. The Egyptian followed us, knowing where we wanted to go. He was obviously serious.

He got in. He stuck to us like a limpet. He gave us a lot of information about the city and tips that weren't in our guidebooks, all without being asked.

Well – we thought, he just wants a decent "bakschisch"
(= tip) from us in the end.
He can have it, as long as he's not intrusive.

He warned us about certain streets we wanted to go into, a particular tram we shouldn't take because there would be problems, etc. The guy really knew his stuff.

He was not only a tour guide, but also our bodyguard. We had not even begged for - what a miracle in Alexandria!

We completed our day's programme, with Mister Egypt always at our side, but not intrusively. Like a shadow in a strange, dangerous city.

I don't want to give all the details of this encounter here, that would be too much.

But it was really exciting. Our thoughts were always between fraud and gratitude, vigilance and enjoyment.

We finally returned to the hotel late in the afternoon, still with our Egyptian shadow in tow. To be honest, now at the end of the tour, it hadn't been that unpleasant having someone with us who knew his way around, and we weren't bothered by other Egyptian traders or beggars.

We thanked the man and said goodbye in front of the hotel, and I wanted to give him a generous baksheesh.

I held out the money for him.

He became annoyed and asked us if we wanted to insult him.

We thought that the baksheesh was not enough for the whole day, so I added a few more notes. He became even more annoyed!

"I don't want any money, accompanying you safely throughout the day is enough for me."

Spoke, turned around and disappeared.

And in the most literal sense. Just gone. Vanished without a trace. In the middle of the pavement.

We finally realised that God had sent us an angel to watch over us, guide us through Alexandria and keep us safe.

Genial! Wonderful! Excellent!

Something similar happened to us in Brazil, where it was a friendly young couple. They even had an old VW Beetle in which we travelled.

In July 2024, we heard another such "angelic belter" from a woman (she is totally credible!) in the church "Esperanza de Vida" in Cala Ratjada, Mallorca. We were there once again to minister and demonstrate the power of God.
It's amazing how many reports of healings and miracles we've already heard and seen there.

This woman reported it publicly in the church, in front of everyone.

She works in room service at a large Apartment Hotel and when she started work the manager came to her and said that she had to prepare eight (!) apartments that day, the guests had left that morning and new guests would arrive the next day. There was no support and not enough staff, she should get on with it, the rooms were pretty "devastated".

That was a shock – order!
Eight flats!
Alone!

Usually, the rooms are left totally grungy and look as if a bomb has hit them. The wet, dirty towels on the floor, the bathroom all smeared, clutter and rubbish everywhere. Everything has to be checked for function and damage. That takes time.
Unfortunately, many hotel guests behave like vandals. After all, they have paid for it.

The woman was completely overstrained by the task, panicked and totally frustrated; she cried out to God and asked for help.

„ GOD, HELP!
Please send me angels to help,
otherwise it can't be done."

She obviously also knew God's emergency number! ☺
It also works from Spain and elsewhere. (and ENGLAND!!!)

She entered the first room that needed to be cleaned with all of her equipment.
It was completely clean and tidy, like something out of a picture book. Almost an exhibition or presentation room.
She looked perplexed and made sure it was the right room →
it was.

Stunned, she stood there and realised that God had truly sent her supernatural help. Angels had already done almost everything.
Functionality: ok!
Completeness: ok!
Bathroom: super – ok!
Apartment overall condition: awesome – ok!

She realised that she only had to make the beds, and that was it. Not even 30 minutes.
The angels had probably not done that, so that she could also tell her boss that she had done something. But the angels do think of everything.

She floated as if on clouds from room 1 to the next. Let's find out what´s waiting for her there.

Hope and faith had grown by leaps and bounds in her heart.

The second room → the same scenario. Like a copy of number 1.
The angels had done a great job again – except for the beds. ☺

Number 2: CHECK - ☺
Number 3: CHECK - ☺
Number 4 to 8: CHECK - ☺

The angels had cleaned all eight rooms. What a miracle. You can believe it or not – Andra and I do because it bears the handwriting of God, is according to the Word of God, and gives glory to God.

God had demonstrated His Word in practice, as it says in Hebrews 1 / 14:
„Are they not all (just) spirits of service, sent to service those who shall inherit salvation????"

Yes, hurray! Super! Logo → the angels! Of course, of course, always happy to do it, more of the same, Lord!

Unfortunately, it is not so brilliant that we often quickly forget such experiences, often not even perceive how God takes care of us.

That is why the Bible urges us not to forget the good deeds of God and to proclaim them. Here it is again as a reminder:

„From David.
*Bless the L*ORD*, O my soul;*
And all that is within me, bless His holy name!
*Bless the L*ORD*, O my soul,*
And forget not all His benefits. "
Psalms 103 / 1 + 2

WONDERS
are not the centre,
Jesus is!

Don't seek the WONDERS itself,
but the One
who gives them – Jesus!

„Come and see the works of God;
He is awesome in His doing
toward the sons of men."
Psalms 66 / 5

Catedral de los Milagros

A visit to a church in Buenos Aires, Argentina, was an experience that left a lasting impression on us.

A few years ago, we were invited to preach there and to pray for people.

„Catedral de los Milagros → Cathedral of Wonders" is how the church named itself.
At first, we thought the name was a bit grandiose, because you often experience that abroad. But far from it!

It was a modern building in the middle of a poor neighbourhood, with mud streets and huge potholes, hills, dirt and rubbish everywhere. And in the middle of it all, like a shining star, an oasis, this church.
New building, lots of glass, everything clean, the lawn and hedges neatly trimmed, security everywhere on the premises and in the building.
Andra and I were each assigned a personal security guard who was always around us and took care of us like guests of the president. VIP!

The worship hall was built for 5,000 people, and there were an estimated 3,500 to 4,000 people there. We were overwhelmed.
There was an air of expectation and joy.

The service begins, first musical part – the visitors sing at the top of their voices and with all their hearts.

After that, one of the pastors comes on stage and opens the so-called "testimony - part."

It is a term that comes from "witness".
Everyone is familiar with the term, for example in front of the police or in court.
"Then I became a witness..." and then you report what you saw, heard and perceived. Facts, personal. No assumptions, no possible conclusions of your own, no – only what you experienced yourself. In the worst case, you will even be sworn to ensure that it is the truth. So pay attention to what you say.

And that's what I'm doing here in the book. It's all true – no need for an oath.

And in the church, people talk about their personal experiences with Jesus. They have become "witnesses to the actions of God" and tell everyone about it in public, that is, they bear "witness" or a "testimony"

One after the other, sometimes entire families, gave testimony of how God had delivered them from an emergency. These were illnesses, financial problems or even dangerous situations, and all of them enthusiastically testified how Jesus had saved them from these situations in a supernatural way. There was a long line of people waiting, everyone wanted to tell their story, and it took about 45 minutes to almost an hour for the pastor to finish this part. Not everyone who was waiting got a chance to tell their story → next time!

I thought that it would somehow continue with the sermon I was supposed to give that day, but far from it.
After these reports from different people, the pastor called for

a decision for Jesus.

I thought to myself, "Wait a minute, they haven't heard the sermon that Jesus loves them and wants to save them." I was somehow stuck in my spiritual thinking and process.

But Jesus did it differently this time. I got my lesson.

People had heard how good God is, that He loves them and that He not only wants to help them in their natural need, but also in their spiritual need.
It was simply a different way of preaching, but no less effective. Perhaps even more effective.

That Jesus went to the cross for every single person, to bear their sins, to forgive their guilt and to open the door back to the Father, so that they could spend an eternity in the presence of God.

„And as Moses lifted up the serpent in the wilderness,
even so must the Son of Man be lifted up,
that whoever believes in Him
should not perish but have eternal life.
For God so loved the world
that He gave His only begotten Son,
that whoever believes in Him should not perish
but have everlasting life.
For God did not send His Son into the world
to condemn the world,
but that the world through Him might be saved."
John 3 / 14 – 17

It was a simple message and at the end of the call, the pastor asked who in the audience wanted to give their life over to Jesus.

„Jesus answered, "Most assuredly, I say to you,
unless one is born of water and the Spirit,
he cannot enter the kingdom of God.
That which is born of the flesh is flesh,
and that which is born of the Spirit is spirit."
John 3 / 5 + 6

To my great astonishment, about 150 people came forward and then went with the pastor and some helpers to an adjoining room, where they were prayed for and it was explained to them what the surrender of their lives to Jesus would mean and how it could and should now continue in their lives as newborn Christians.

I was truly amazed at how God had used these reports of supernatural activity to touch people's hearts and draw them to Jesus.

This had a lasting influence on my life and also on our ministry in the church and in other nations.

Now we knew why the church is called the "Cathedral of Miracles". They happen here all the time and people talk about them.
They have this period of "testimonies" in every service, and every time, 100 to 200 people decide to follow Jesus.
Hallelujah.

Imagine if that were the order of the day in every church, no matter what its name or denomination.
in every nation, millions of people would come to Jesus in one year.
WOW!

And shall I tell you something, or better yet, prophesy?

THERE WILL COME SUCH A TIME!

Because God has promised it.

I preached about the power of God and healing. Power and miracles belong together and are a character of God. Jesus demonstrated this a hundred thousand times during his ministry here on earth.

> *„And there are also many other things that Jesus did,*
> *which if they were written one by one,*
> *I suppose that even the world itself could not contain*
> *the books that would be written. Amen."*
> John 21 / 25

> *The apostle Paul writes:*
> *„Now some are puffed up,*
> *as though I were not coming to you.*
> *But I will come to you shortly, if the Lord wills,*
> **and I will know, not the word of those who are puffed up,**
> **but the power.**
> **For the kingdom of God is not in word but in power."**
> 1 Corinthians 4 / 18 - 20

Paul is very clear here about what it is about!

The power of God, the Holy Spirit.
Power always becomes visible,
in the case of God through signs, wonders, healings and
deliverance.

He wasn't interested in the blah-blah, the clever words or dry sermons that starve people on the long arm or only give them a meagre diet. They didn't really get to know the God of miracles. It was bound to be an interesting confrontation. I would have loved to have been there, playing the fly on the wall.

You should know the inventor and creator of the word "wonder"!

Whether you see it that way or not, that's the way the Bible sees it.
That is how God sees it.
That is how Jesus sees it.
That is how the Holy Spirit sees it.
Me and many others see it the same way. ☺

Back to Argentina. When the invitation to pray was given, people came to the front in droves and the Holy Spirit touched so many with healings, deliverance, new strength, prayers in tongues and much more. It was like the early church in the New Testament. Glorious and wonderful.

It took us a long time to pray for them all. Remember how many had come.

I hope and believe that Jesus will give us another opportunity to visit this church, to learn, to hear and see miracles, and to serve there.

Something like that ignites your faith turbo!
The afterburner! The "Fast and Furious of faith"!
A film should be made about that. It would be great.

Feurio!

In 1995, I went to the police academy for two years to study and get into the higher police force.

So we decided to get a second, simple car so that Andra would also be mobile during the week, because I was away from Monday to Friday.

I prayed about it and asked Jesus for a suitable vehicle so that I could make use of these two years of study.
At the time, I was doing police service in the town of Forchheim and I needed a spare part for my Golf. So, before I went on duty, I drove to a car recycler in Forchheim, got my used spare part and then I saw that he had three cars in his yard that still looked quite good and were still complete.

The car recycler had placed notes behind the windscreen that apparently contained prices.

One vehicle in particular caught my eye: a red, four-door Talbot, a good old "French swing". The note said "200". (Most French cars used to have very soft suspension, so you sat on a comfortable couch. I don't know how it is today.)

I asked the boss if the car was roadworthy or if it was to be scrapped.
"Nah, it's OK, roadworthy, just a bit old, no MOT."

"And it's supposed to cost 200 marks, or is there a zero missing?" I asked him.

"No, no, that's all right. Just 200 Deutschmarks")

I examined the vehicle, found no serious defects, hardly any rust, and asked the boss if I could take it for a test drive. That was possible. Red numbers on it, entered in the logbook and I drove off, put the speedster through its paces.

I let the „Frenchman" rock properly.

Everything seemed to be in order. So I went straight to the Car Inspection Station to have it inspected.

I knew the Car Inspection boss.

"The car is fine. No defects. Amazing. Do you want to buy the car? If not, I'll buy it."

Well, when an expert tells you that, your heart leaps for joy. I immediately had the relevant test reports drawn up, paid and drove back to the yard.

"Sold!" and I held out 100 marks to him as a deposit. "I don't have any more on me now. The rest when I pick it up."

The boss looked at me a bit askance and said: "Knowing you, you've even been to the Car Inspection." "Of course. Without defects."

He gave me the papers, I registered the car and picked it up three days later, paid the rest and drove enthusiastically, totally grateful, praising and totally happy home. God had given me the appropriate "study car".

I was on the autobahn, driving towards Bamberg. I was relaxed in my "French swing", humming a song of praise to God's goodness, blessings and provision, when suddenly thick black smoke billowed out from under the dashboard. It kept getting more and more, getting denser and denser, and suddenly flames shot out of the instrument panel.

„ The scrapheap is now burning,
what kind of junk have you bought?
Your stupid trust in God – now you have the mess!
Bye-Bye – blessing!"

A malicious voice tried to persuade me and laughed at me.
I said loudly:

> „ But that can't be!
> That's not the voice of my Lord Jesus!
> I know it very well.
> He never talks to me like that."

I knew immediately that this was a spiritual confrontation. Victory or defeat. Jesus or devil, blessing or harm. French swing or burnt-out scrap heap.

And I boldly used the authority of the name of Jesus in faith!

> „ Fire, go out – in Jesus' name!
> This is my car, my gift from God
> and, devil, you will not take it away from me and destroy it.
> Get out, get your dirty fingers off my car.
> In the name of Jesus!!!!"

It happened in a second. A spontaneous reaction of faith, without much thought.

Of course, I also know that you normally pull over to the right, turn on the hazard warning lights, jump out and then let the car burn. There would have been no other option. There was no fire extinguisher on board. There was no mobile phone, the fire brigade would have taken too long.

But it literally burst out of me. I knew the devil wanted to rob me of my blessing and I would not allow it.

I'm saying it was my reaction.
Please don't just imitate me just because I did it that way.
You also have to have faith to do it.
So check your faith first, then act!
And that applies in principle.

"In the name of Jesus! Fire, go out!"

The flames went out immediately, the black smoke smelling of rubber and plastic diminished and then stopped altogether. I opened the windows to air the car and then I praised and shouted for joy to my Jesus and the power of his name. The name of Jesus and HIS word had once again proven to be powerful and true.

„So Jesus answered and said to them:
Assuredly, I say to you,
if you have faith and do not doubt,
you will not only do what was done to the fig tree,
but also if you say to this mountain,
Be removed and be cast into the sea,
it will be done. "
Matthew 21 / 21

Jesus:
"Have faith – don't doubt – speak to the mountain →
it happens and jump into the sea!"

Günther:
"Have faith – don't doubt – speak to the fire → it happens and goes out!"

It's kind of logical. When the mountain throws itself into the sea, it sinks. Normal process of gravity.
If you throw the fire into the sea, it goes out.
Any more questions?

And You:
????

The car ran perfectly for two years, without any problems, and reliably took me to and from university, and even to a

212

skiing holiday in South Tyrol / Italy. After the two years, we no longer needed it, the MOT had expired again, and I drove it back to the car recycler's yard, where I had bought it. The scrap price was high and I got → DM 200 for it.
Hallelujah!!!!

"Jesus said to him:
If you can believe?
all things are possible to him
who believes. *"*
Mark 9 / 23

It is almost impossible
to carry the torch of truth
through a crowd without
scorching someone's beard.
Georg Christoph Lichtenberg
1742 - 1799, physicist, natural scientist, mathematician, author

Faith is love for the invisible,
trust in the impossible,
the implausible.
Johann Wolfgang von Goethe
1749 - 1832, German poet, politician, naturalist

It never stops:

At the end of a book, you usually read "in conclusion" or "last but not least" or something similar, and you mean that it actually stops and is over now.

But that is only partly true. Of course the book ends at some point, it has to.
But the message lives on.

The wonders continue.

God continues → with you and me.

From glory to glory.
From victory to victory.
From positive experience to positive experience.
From wonder to wonder.
Until we arrive in eternity with HIM and are able to see what we had believed and hoped for.

But until then, I want to experience as many miracles and powerful manifestations as possible. There is still so much that Jesus has promised that I have not yet experienced, but it is possible because Jesus said it.

For example, RESURRECTION!

My, my, my! This is exciting.

When I was still in the police force, I often had to deal with death. Accident victims, natural causes, and sometimes, when I was alone with the deceased, I would start to pray.
Not for the dead, we've already had that, it's no use anymore.

But I began to call them back to life. I laid my hands on

them. I proclaimed my commission from John 14:12, but unfortunately nothing happened so far.
So there is still plenty of room for growth.
And I will not give up!

I still don't understand many things, but that doesn't stop me from doing what the word of God says, what I should do.
It is not written anywhere that I have to understand it beforehand. Which brings us back to "logic".

Jesus did not say, "whoever believes in me and understands everything...", but only, "Whoever believes in me..."

We are too "success-oriented".
We have learnt that when we do something, we look at the result.
Good result → we continue, repeat it, it worked.
Bad result → we try a few more times and then we stop.
Result "0" → we don't continue at all, it's no use, it doesn't work.

And unfortunately, we often apply this principle in our faith as well.
We pray once or twice, don't see an immediate change or improvement, and we stop, probably it wasn't God's will.

But faith works differently.
Faith is not "results-oriented" but simply "Jesus-said-it-and-I'm-doing-it-oriented"!

I do it trusting in HIM, His word. I am obedient and I am curious to see when the result will come. That is HIS work, when and how Jesus does it. I don't block myself.

We have experienced it so often: we have prayed with someone for healing, he and we felt nothing, saw and noticed nothing.

Give up? Sorry, no luck this time? No way!
Keep believing and trusting.
We prayed with all our faith because Jesus said we should do it.
And very often, the healing occurred hours, the next day or the week.
Hallelujah.

Jesus is not a chewing gum machine. Pray once and immediately get the result. That is not confidence, not faith in Jesus. Sometimes Jesus waits a little to see if we will hold on to HIM, faith in prayer and trust in the power of the word of God. Therefore, do not panic!

Jesus stands by HIS word. After all, HE said it.
And we trust HIM to do it because HE said it.
Everything easy, Alles Paletti, gut*!

Raising the dead, for example, is totally illogical. Dead is dead. Any doctor will tell you that, and logic, of course. And that's why we're not even trying anymore.
Logic is holding us in its firm grip.

Logic leaves no room for other possibilities.

But with Jesus, it's different.
He raises Lazarus who has been dead for four days. So it's not a case of "apparently dead" and "oops – the doctor was wrong". The process of decomposition, a so-called "sure sign of death", was already well underway. The Bible tells us that "he had already smelt bad". In other words: ponged, stank. You know what it means.
And Jesus brings him back. Imagine that. It's like running the

film backwards. Decay in reverse, fly larvae back, foul smell gone again, the engine starts again, brain dead → reset and running again, without brain damage.

Lazarus leaps out of his tomb again like a mummy, wrapped in shrouds.

Logic goes crazy, screams, feels existential panic, and can't get 1 + 1 together anymore. Feels passed over and ignored (it was, too ☺) A total logic breakdown.

And that only because Jesus, in the certainty of faith, calls: "Lazarus, come out!"

Jesus told his disciples: "Speak to the mountain..." (remember?)
And so HE has no problem doing it himself.
HE just speaks to Lazarus... and he comes.
And to the wind and to the waves and to sickness, to demons
and and and and and and so on.

Do you understand? Do you see what is missing today? Let's do it again!

With Jesus it is logical. HE is aware of the Kingdom of God and his power and different principles. Faith is not earthly grounded, but heavenly.
With "heavenly logic", it is clear that when God, Jesus, the Holy Spirit and the person who believes in Jesus (you and me) say something in faith, it happens. No matter how. It happens.

> *„Then God said, Let there be light;*
> *and there was light "*
> Genesis 1 / 3

Of course – logical!

God believes what he says and faith brings forth things that do not yet actually exist.

Have you ever noticed that God does not make the sun here? That comes later. The sun, moon and stars make their grand debut in verses 14 to 19.

Now the question: What kind of light was it that God spoke into existence?
Pondering – pondering – and studying → the word of God.

I might give you the answer in another book that I might write. Until then, you'll have to be patient or better you ask Jesus for an answer.

> *„Now faith is the substance of things hoped for,*
> *the evidence of things not seen.*
>
> *By faith we understand*
> *that the worlds were framed by the word of God,*
> *so that the things which are seen*
> *were not made of things which are visible."*
> Hebrews 11 / 1 + 3

Faith in Jesus is the be-all and end-all. And faith often has nothing to do with logic.
Miracles are illogical – and yet they happen (PRAISE GOD) millions of times.

Finally, a few examples from our experience of when we prayed for people with this faith, in brief. You may find the full version in the book "Acts 29".

Argentina – a young man – a gang member – shootout – he has 5 bullets in his spine – inoperable, wheelchair, life-long paraplegic – prayer – he walks again, goodbye wheelchair – with five "reminder bullets" in his spine, decided for Jesus –

no more gang.

Brazil. Young woman. Terminal cancer. Nothing but skin and bones, with only a few weeks left to live. Prayer. We see her again a year later. A beautiful, vibrant woman. Full of life!

Germany – older woman – neurological, incurable problem – mobility increasingly limited – unable to climb stairs, difficult with walking frame, on the verge of a wheelchair and house conversion – prayer – runs up and down stairs again, etc.

Mallorca – a young girl jumps from the second floor – crushed, pulverised foot – wheelchair for life – prayer – immediately walking normally again and now giving healing interviews with her parents – for the glory of Jesus.

That and more is what we experience with Jesus. You can find a whole bunch of reports like this on our church website at:

www.jesus-gemeinde.de/aktuelles/heilungsberichte

Why doesn't it always happen the way we want it to? No idea. It's God's business. But we're working on it and in the meantime we're just doing it. Logic, understanding or results or not!

Whether it's a "great" miracle or an annoying headache - we jump for joy, cheer, rejoice, are endlessly grateful, reverent, worshipful, amazed because of

Jesus

I must and will trust Jesus. HIS word. That HE will take care of it in due time, I will learn more faith.

„Jesus said to her,
Did I not say to you that if you would believe
you would see the glory of God?"
John 11 / 40

„Then Jesus said to the centurion,
Go your way; and as you have believed,
so let it be done for you.
And his servant was healed that same hour."
Matthew 8 / 13

„But Jesus turned around, and when He saw her He said,
Be of good cheer, daughter;
your faith has made you well.
And the woman was made well from that hour."
Matthew 9 / 22

„Then Jesus said to him,
Go your way; your faith has made you well.
And immediately he received his sight
and followed Jesus on the road."
Mark 10 / 52

The Bible is full of it.
Faith – healings – deliverances – wonders – mighty demonstrations of God – without end, without limit. Anything is possible, logic or no logic.

„Jesus said to him,
If you can believe,
all things are possible to him who believes."
Mark 9 / 23

And that is what we pursue. No matter what our personal circumstances are. No matter what logic or "theology" says. No matter what people say.
What Jesus says is important to me. And He says it very clearly:

„And when He had called His twelve disciples to Him,
He gave them power over unclean spirits, to cast them out,
and to heal all kinds of sickness and all kinds of disease."
Matthew 10 / 1

„And as you go, preach, saying,
The kingdom of heaven is at hand.
Heal the sick,
cleanse the lepers,
raise the dead,
cast out demons.
Freely you have received, freely give."
Matthew 10 / 7 + 8

(other Bible scriptures show that other followers of Jesus had also received this authority, not only the twelve apostles. e.g. Luke 10 / 1; John 14 / 12...)

And now the whole thing again in the personalised form, to be read out loud, proclaimed, entering the brain and heart, somewhat annoying to logic, but in the scripturally correct form:
(this is now the "Günther translation"; you are welcome to use your own name!)

„ And **JESUS** called his disciple GÜNTHER to him
and gave him power over unclean spirits,
(Yeeah – the real Ghostbuster)
so that GÜNTHER would
cast out demons and heal every disease and every infirmity."
(based loosely on Matthew 10 / 1)

"**JESUS** said to GÜNTHER.
But go and preach, saying:
The kingdom of heaven is at hand.
GÜNTHER – heal the sick, (Amen!)
GÜNTHER – raise the dead, (oops!)
GÜNTHER – cleanse lepers, (?)
GÜNTHER – cast out demons. (Yee-ha!)
You received it for free,
give it for free."
(based loosely on Matthew 10:7-8)

„ Verily, verily, GÜNTHER, I say to you:
If you believe in me, **Jesus**,
you, GÜNTHER, will do the works that I do.

Yes, GÜNTHER, imagine,
even greater than these,
because I am going back to my Father
and entrust you with the continuation of my work."
(based loosely on John 14 / 12)

Do you notice the momentum that the word takes on when
you read it with your name in it? How it literally takes you
away?
You see, that's what you can do with the word of God, you
should take it → personally. Otherwise it's easy to be left out,
because it concerns the others.

But that's how I realise: I'M THE ONE MEANT!

And I experience it more and more, stronger and stronger and it will be without limit because Jesus says so. HIS defined, ACHIEVABLE standard is

ALL – without limits

Are you in?
Have I whetted your appetite a little for trusting in Jesus more?
Have I been able to entice you out of your previous, sometimes unsatisfying, boring way of being a Christian?
Are you motivated to get to know the God of the Bible and experience him as never before?
To finally begin the adventure of a lifetime in faith or to continue it more intensely?
To serve People with the strength and the word of God with healing, deliverance and miracles?
We don't have much time left! Jesus is coming back soon. MARANATHA!

I hope and pray that I have succeeded to some extent.

And then one day, when we meet again in eternity at the last, we will sit around a heavenly campfire and tell each other what we have experienced with Jesus. Our eyes will keep returning to the ONE sitting with us around the campfire, smiling lovingly and listening enthusiastically to what we are telling HIM.
And HE gives us HIS commentary on it, explaining the spiritual background to it that we didn't even see or check.

And us, me and you, HE puts HIS warm, pierced hand on our shoulder and says: "Well done boys, well done girls"

And then we will have reached our destination,
with our beloved Jesus,
in the arms of our Heavenly Father
and the surrounding presence of the Holy Spirit
in HIS eternal, WONDER – ful Kingdom.

So Andra and I will say goodbye, adieu, adela, (= Bamberg slang) good bye, hasta pronto!

We have to go on, there is no time to lose, there is still so much for us to learn, discover and experience, so many WONDERS to see and pass on.

And don't tell us now there aren't any

Wonders!

Think about, pray about and write down where you have experienced miracles in your own life that you can recognise as miracles after reading the book.

Resolve to tell at least 10 people in one month about the miracle you experienced with Jesus, and pray for it.

Read the Book of Acts and see how many people came to believe in Jesus because of ONE miracle. You will be surprised.

Natural – Supernatural
The Restoration of the Supernatural Church

At these conferences, we invite guest speakers who can say something on this topic and have practical experience.

The aim is to draw the participants' attention to areas of the Bible that have been forgotten, neglected or misunderstood. They are encouraged to engage with the signs and wonders of the Bible and the early church. They are motivated to study the Word of God with the help of the Holy Spirit, to put it into practice, to receive the fire of the Holy Spirit and to experience it.

The participants come from Germany (claro), various European countries, but also from South America, the USA, etc., with different church backgrounds, but mostly from the free church sector.

Participation is free of charge, with no need to register in writing. Further information and dates can be found on the homepage of the Jesus Gemeinde Bamberg.

www.jesus-gemeinde.de → Conferences

A warm welcome!   Herzlich willkommen!

Bienvenidos!

Добро пожаловать!   !أهلاً وسهلاً بك

Bem-vindo!   欢迎光临   Üdvözöljük!

Acts 29

I mentioned in the book that I wrote my first book in 2015. It is full of personal experiences of healing and deliverance. The aim of the book is to trust in the power of Jesus and to expect that He will still do miracles today according to His word. If He has done it once, He can and will do it again. If He has done it for someone else, He can and will do it for you too.

God's miracles are for all who reach out for Him.

Günther Kunstmann

Acts 29
Signs and Wonders -
they still happen!

**The adventurous journey in God's dimension
Reports of what Jesus is doing today**

A book of motivation and facts

This book describes in an easy-to-understand way how Jesus performs miracles in people's lives. Even today. Amazing reports that inspire and motivate, that cause us to marvel and hope, and that rekindle our own faith in Jesus. Questions, arguments, and obstacles to God's supernatural work are examined, as is the simple realisation and statement:

Nothing is impossible for Jesus.

Personal experiences and life changes will encourage you to see your own situation in a new light and to tackle and change it in the power of Jesus.

The book simply shows that miracles have not ceased, but are still happening. For you too! Study Jesus and HIS word and you will see that HE performed so many miracles, healing all possible and impossible kinds of illnesses. No disease and no demonic power was safe from HIM. HE showed the love of God in action.

The book has 136 pages and costs €9.99
(Price in Germany)
It was published by BOD-Verlag Norderstedt.
ISBN-Nr: 978-3741250552
and available also from other online merchants,

e.g. AMAZON, ...
also as an e-book! ☺

With Jesus on patrol

The second book I published in 2018 has the promising title:

with Jesus on patrol
and the power of prayer in action
Experiences from my police service

It deals with the understanding of faith and authority as shown to us in the Bible. How and where do I use the authority in the name of Jesus? What a powerful responsibility Jesus has given us.
Often we ask God to do something in a difficult situation, but HE apparently does not act.
Because HE has given us the task. We should become active for HIM here on earth, for HIM. In HIS name.

The book tells in an entertaining but profound way how Jesus can be present and miracles can happen even in the more than 40 years of service of a police officer. So-called police-official miracles.

What powerful prayer can achieve and how it can help make police investigations a success.
Amazing reports and experiences that inspire and motivate, lead to wonder, hope and prayer, and re-activate one's own position as a Christian and one's role in society.

Ended a series of accidents and burglaries series, blown drug rings and caught major dealers, all these things experienced in the police force and much more are told in this book.
Connections with biblical truths, practical implementation in prayer and the dangers of passive Christianity are also shown.

A call for all disciples of Jesus to pray!
Transform your city and country through the authority of faith.
Nothing is impossible for Jesus!

The book has 192 pages and costs €12.00
(Price in Germany)
It was published by BOD-Verlag Norderstedt.
ISBN-Nr: 978-3753420783
and available also from other online merchants,

e.g. AMAZON, ...
also again - as an e-book! ☺

These books are also available in German (logo) and Spanish.

Have fun and gain many valuable insights while reading, and have amazing experiences while practising!

Finally,

And yet, WONDERS
are the handwriting of God.
They are part of HIS love letter
to YOU!
Recognise them in your life.
Big and small wonders!

Finding Jesus
is the greatest WONDER
one can experience for oneself.

Forgiveness of sins, grace,
being accepted
and born again
are greater WONDERS
than anything we have told YOU
about in this book.

And now there is only one thing left for us to say:

You will experience incredible things
that you can tell your grandchildren one day.
Or if you don't want to wait that long,
tell everyone at every appropriate opportunity.
For the Glory of Jesus.

Start expecting WONDERS.
Because we have a God of WONDERS
as Lord and Father!

**Don't believe everything your logic says,
but believe everything the word of God says.**

And be honest with yourself:
We do not yet know everything about the kingdom of God
and we have to and should be open,
that the Holy Spirit can lead us further -
into HIS dimension.

We pray for you, dear reader,
that you will be totally touched and encouraged
by Jesus
and experience amazing encounters and
WONDERS.

Be blessed
in the name of Jesus!

Günther & Andra Kunstmann
Bamberg, 2024